What people are saying about …

DOES THE BIBLE
SUPPORT SAME-SEX
MARRIAGE?

"Another splendid book from Preston Sprinkle, who manages to address some of the toughest contemporary issues with a light but vital touch. There is a wealth of important material here in short and accessible form."

Rt. Rev. Prof. N. T. Wright, (former Bishop of Durham), professor emeritus of New Testament at University of St Andrews, senior research fellow at Wycliffe Hall, Oxford

"For any conversation to go anywhere, what we need is not only compassion but clarity. Preston displays both in his ministry and especially in this resource. His lived experience with the LGBTQ community, along with the theological depth he holds, makes this book a necessity."

Jackie Hill Perry, Bible teacher and author of *Gay Girl, Good God*

"If we care about people, then we must be thinking critically, theologically, and extremely lovingly about the issues of sexuality today. How do we know what is true or not? As emotional human beings, we are easily swayed by watching enough ninety-second convincing TikTok videos which may or may not be true. In this book we have a guide to sorting through and looking at big questions based on very important and trustworthy Bible study methods and a premise that all the Scriptures are all inspired by God. But not only do we have the theology and depth behind the answers given, we also have pastoral, sensitive, kind, and caring responses. I am extremely grateful for this book."

Dan Kimball, author of *How (Not) To Read the Bible*, vice president and associate professor at Western Seminary

"The Bible shows time and time again that when Jesus walked among us, he did so as one who was "full of grace *and* truth." As recipients *of* his grace and truth, Jesus's most grateful followers have sought likewise to embody a similar posture toward their neighbors. Undergirded with conviction *and* compassion, compelled by law *and* love, and having the courage and kindness to speak warnings *and* welcome, this posture is both a calling and a privilege for us who call ourselves "Christian." In giving sound advice about how to flex all of these God-honoring, neighbor-loving muscles all at once, I can think of no better guide than my friend Preston Sprinkle."

Scott Sauls, senior pastor of Christ Presbyterian Church, author of *Jesus Outside the Lines* and *Beautiful People Don't Just Happen*

"He's done it again! Preston is my favorite go-to voice when it comes to treating the toughest questions around sexuality with both theological depth and pastoral heart. This book will not only help you understand the top arguments around same-sex marriage, but it will equip you to have these conversations well. Preston brings scholarly rigor that's easy to read while calling all of us who follow Jesus to be countercultural in both our conviction and our compassion. I'm so grateful that Preston's leading so many of us in this conversation; once you read this book, you'll be too."

Josh Butler, lead pastor of Redemption Tempe

"This is a very useful and informative resource for anyone wanting to understand the arguments supporting an affirmative view of gay marriage. Preston does a masterful job of combining biblical scholarship, historical evidence, current trends, and personal compassion in his responses."

Juli Slattery, PsyD, president and
cofounder of Authentic Intimacy

"Preston Sprinkle does not shy away from the hard questions about Christianity, sexuality, and marriage. Sprinkle lays out a clear, compelling, and compassionate case as to why historical Christianity affirms that marriage is between one man and one woman in life-long commitment to each other. In a world where 'love is love,' Sprinkle offers a counter-cultural case for Christian marriage."

Michael F. Bird, PhD, academic dean and lecturer in
New Testament at Ridley College, Melbourne, Australia

"In this important new resource, Preston Sprinkle addresses common objections many have regarding historic Christian teaching about sexuality in a winsome, compassionate, and even disarming manner. Unlike similar books, however, Sprinkle's deep affirmation of the humanity and dignity of LGBTQ+ people permeates his reflections. Christians who adopt a posture like Sprinkle's in this discussion will not only be more faithful to Scripture, but they will also be more like Jesus."

Nate Collins, PhD, president and founder
of Revoice, author of *All But Invisible*

"You can tell you're reading a good book when you immediately want multiple copies to distribute as widely as possible. This is such a book. Preston doesn't just know and explain the various arguments when it comes to the Bible and same-sex marriage, but he clearly loves the precious people most involved too, which is such a rare but necessary combination."

Ed Shaw, ministry director, www.livingout.org,
author of *Purposeful Sexuality*

DOES THE BIBLE SUPPORT SAME-SEX MARRIAGE?

DOES THE BIBLE SUPPORT SAME-SEX MARRIAGE?

21 CONVERSATIONS FROM A HISTORICALLY CHRISTIAN VIEW

NEW YORK TIMES BESTSELLING AUTHOR

Preston Sprinkle

DAVID C COOK

transforming lives together

DOES THE BIBLE SUPPORT SAME-SEX MARRIAGE?
Published by David C Cook
4050 Lee Vance Drive
Colorado Springs, CO 80918 U.S.A.

Integrity Music Limited, a Division of David C Cook
Brighton, East Sussex BN1 2RE, England

The graphic circle C logo is a registered trademark of David C Cook.

Library of Congress Control Number 2022951926
ISBN 978-0-8307-8567-4
eISBN 978-0-8307-8577-3

© 2023 Preston Sprinkle

The Team: Michael Covington, Greg Coles, Stephanie Bennett, Judy
Gillispie, Kayla Fenstermaker, James Hershberger, Susan Murdock
Cover Design: Micah Kandros

Printed in the United States of America
First Edition 2023

1 2 3 4 5 6 7 8 9 10

041223

CONTENTS

PREFACE

Over the last ten years, I've spent a good chunk of my life engaging the LGBTQ conversation. What started as a research project figuring out what the Bible says about same-sex sexual relationships has led to a full-time ministry where I'm constantly exploring ways to help the church embody both truth and grace in the LGBTQ conversation. Part of my ministry involves speaking to people about the topic. And whenever I speak, I always leave room for Q and A. Oh, the questions I've received! Some of them are biblical; others are relational; still others have to do with church policies. Some questions are off the wall or seem designed to corner me in a trap. I honestly love these Q and A times, even though they can be quite stressful. Over the years, I've kept a mental list of some of the most frequently asked questions. And that's where this book comes in.

This book addresses some of the most frequently asked questions in the conversation about same-sex sexuality. More specifically, this book addresses the most common pushbacks to the traditional view of marriage and sexuality. I haven't addressed all of them in this book; to do so would require a much larger tome. But I have addressed some of the most common or most compelling ones.

You need to know up front that this book is incomplete. That is, if you've never read a book on the LGBTQ conversation, then please return this one and pick up a different one. Amazon has a great return policy—you'll get your money back. This book is *not* designed to be a holistic, pastoral, and relational treatment of the topic.[1] This book also isn't going to deal with the transgender conversation, which involves a whole host of questions beyond those of sexuality.[2] And this book certainly isn't a personal story about what it's like being gay, because that isn't my story.[3]

This book has a narrower focus. It's designed to offer thoughtful Christian responses to some of the main arguments for same-sex marriage. I do think such theological issues play an important role in the conversation. Many of the questions we'll wrestle with in the pages to come are questions Christians have asked me over and over again through the years. While people can scour several books to piece together responses to all the questions we'll deal with, I've yet to find an easily accessible one-stop-shop book that contains responses to some of the most important critiques of the traditional view of marriage.

---

1. There are several other books that I can highly recommend, including Nate Collins, *All But Invisible: Exploring Identity Questions at the Intersection of Faith, Gender, and Sexuality* (Grand Rapids, MI: Zondervan, 2017), and anything by Mark Yarhouse on the topic. My own attempt to write such a book is *People to Be Loved: Why Homosexuality Is Not Just an Issue* (Grand Rapids, MI: Zondervan, 2015).

2. I wrestle with a lot of these questions in my book *Embodied: Transgender Identities, the Church, and What the Bible Has to Say* (Colorado Springs: David C Cook, 2021).

3. There are a lot of great books written from the perspective of someone who is gay or same-sex attracted. Some of my personal favorites are Greg Coles, *Single, Gay, Christian: A Personal Journey of Faith and Sexual Identity* (Downers Grove, IL: IVP Press, 2017); Wesley Hill, *Washed and Waiting: Reflections on Christian Faithfulness and Homosexuality* (Grand Rapids, MI: Zondervan, 2016); and Jackie Hill Perry, *Gay Girl, Good God: The Story of Who I Was and Who God Has Always Been* (Nashville: B&H Publishing, 2018).

This book is written for three groups of Christians. First, I'm writing to Christians who hold a traditional view of marriage and yet find themselves in conversations with people who don't. You might not know what to say when you're asked, "Don't you know that the Bible has been mistranslated by homophobic Christians who made the Bible anti-gay?" Or you might not have a solid response if someone says, "When the Bible prohibits gay sex, it's not talking about consensual relationships." This book is designed to help you think through these and other questions with biblical fidelity and grace.

I'm also writing for Christians who don't really know what they believe about marriage and sexuality. Maybe you've dabbled in both sides of the debate and walked away not sure what to believe. I hope this book will help you in your journey.

For those of you who are committed to an affirming view of same-sex marriage, I haven't forgotten about you. I hope you feel honored as a person as you read this book, because I've tried hard to make sure I'm representing your view with honesty and integrity. Even if we still end up disagreeing with each other in the end, I'd love it if you read this book from a place of curiosity and charity. We'll talk more about that posture in Foundation 1.

A quick word about language: I freely use the terms *gay* and *lesbian*, rather than exclusively using the more conservative term *same-sex attracted*. There's a debate within Christianity about whether Christians should ever call themselves gay or use the phrase "gay Christian." I'm well aware of this debate, but this book is not about sorting all this out. (I do touch on it briefly in

Conversation 21.) For now, just know that I'm using the terms *gay* and *lesbian* to mean "attracted to the same sex," regardless of whether such persons *are* having gay sex or even believe in same-sex marriage. Nothing more should be read into my use of the terms *gay* and *lesbian* than that I'm referring to a person who is attracted to the same sex.

However, I'm not going to use the acronym LGBTQ as a synonym for *gay*, as many people do (and as I've done in the past). Once we go past LGB (lesbian, gay, bisexual), we're dealing with a rather different set of questions—questions that aren't necessarily about sexuality (though Q, queer, could include this). T, or trans*, in particular is an almost entirely different conversation. Some trans* people are straight; others are gay; others are bisexual; still others are asexual. In itself, LGB has little to do with T, even if some T people are also LGB. Since this book is about marriage and same-sex sexual relationships, I won't be dealing with questions around transgender identities. Sometimes the term LGBTQ might be appropriate, if we're talking about the general experiences that gender and sexual minorities have had in the church; in this case, there's a lot of commonality. But unless I really do intend to refer to lesbians, gay people, bisexual people, transgender people, *and* queer people, I won't use the acronym LGBTQ.

In the pages that follow, I'm going to summarize and respond to twenty-one different arguments *against* the traditional view of marriage. But before we get to these arguments, there are two important preliminary foundations that will set the stage for everything that follows. The first foundation is about how we should go about having these conversations—or *any* contentious conversation. Please, do not skip this chapter. I put it first for a reason. The second foundation sums up the historically Christian view of marriage; it's important to know what this view even is before we discuss arguments against it.

After that, we'll survey twenty-one arguments (or, as I call them, conversations). Many of these conversations are interconnected, and I've tried to link them in a way that flows logically from one chapter to the next. For this reason, I'd recommend reading this book from cover to cover like you would with most books. However, I have written each individual conversation in such a way that it can stand alone. So if you want, you can flip to a particular argument that catches your eye. If you do this, please do read Foundations 1 and 2 no matter what. The rest of the book won't make sense unless you do.

Be aware up front that a few of these conversations are quite technical and involve debates about Greek words, Greco-Roman culture, and scholarly stuff that lives primarily in the stuffy halls of academia. (Conversations 4, 5, and 7 are among the heaviest.) Even as I engage these conversations, I'll try to do so in an accessible way so those unfamiliar with the background of the debate can still follow along. I want to be intellectually responsible by not avoiding tough arguments, while still writing in such a way that people without PhDs can understand.

Before we jump in, I want to acknowledge that many of you reading this aren't attracted to the same sex and so there's a distance between you and the content of this book. I'm in the same boat. I've only ever been attracted to the opposite sex. If this describes you, then please note: Learning how to navigate the biblical and theological arguments surrounding same-sex marriage is important, but if that's all you do, it's woefully insufficient. Christ-followers are called to embody the presence of Christ in this conversation. Don't read this book unless you're also willing to live a life that eagerly welcomes gay people into it.

If you're attracted to the same sex, then you're probably reading this book with a bit more investment. Maybe you're considering adopting a view that affirms same-sex marriage for Christians, or you're wondering if the traditional view truly has merit. Wherever you're at in your journey, I'm thankful that you want to dive deeper into questions about faith and sexuality. Reading a book about same-sex sexuality by a straight guy might make you roll your eyes, and I don't blame you. But I want you to know that I've tried to be as sensitive as I can in speaking about a topic that I don't personally experience. I did make sure that several gay and same-sex attracted Christians read through this book before it was published. They helped me fix the unintentionally insensitive things written in earlier drafts (yes, there were a few!). I take full ownership of any mistakes that remain.

I hope that all my readers, in agreement or disagreement, will do two things after reading this book: think more deeply and love more widely. Every Christian reader can agree that we all could use a good dose of both.

HOW TO HAVE
A FRUITFUL
CONVERSATION

INTRODUCTION

Before we discuss same-sex marriage, we need to talk about how to have a fruitful conversation.

I used to think that good conversations happened only when two people agreed. But a profitable conversation is not one where everyone has to agree; that would be unrealistic and not always helpful. A profitable conversation, rather, is one where everyone feels understood and honored—even if disagreement remains. Unprofitable conversations are ones where people aren't actually listening to what others are saying; where both sides focus on defending their viewpoint rather than exploring what's actually true; where people feel more degraded and angrier when the conversation is over.

Truly profitable conversations happen when both parties are genuinely curious about the other person's view, embody a humble posture in the dialogue, and try to understand where someone is coming from. The quality of our beliefs is obviously important. But the manner in which we hold to those beliefs can be equally important. Sometimes *how* we believe is just as important as *what* we believe.

Some people might disagree with my last statement. I know, because I used to be one of those people. I used to think that if the content of what I believed was true, then all I needed to do was declare it to others. The manner in which I held to my beliefs didn't really matter. If what I was saying was true, and if others genuinely cared about the truth, then I figured they would believe it too. But I've come to realize that this isn't how belief works. We don't believe things simply because we add up all the facts and rationally form our beliefs from those facts. Facts are important, but humans are complex beings, with stories and emotions and thick interpretive lenses colored by our unique life experiences. Simply declaring facts to people rarely convinces them that what you're saying is true, unless they *want* what you're saying to be true.

I'll never forget speaking on sexuality at a college chapel service several years ago. Half my talk defended the traditional view of marriage (one man and one woman), and the other half addressed how the church should love gay people better. After the talk, a student confronted me for teaching *against* a biblical view of marriage. With her Bible open to Leviticus 18:22—a verse I had actually quoted in the message—she told me that this verse (among many others) disagreed with my alleged defense of same-sex marriage. She didn't seem to realize that my talk had defended traditional marriage. Another student came up to me right after her and asked, "Why do you hate gay people so much?" He didn't seem to realize that half my message was all about loving and delighting in and listening to and learning from gay people.

One message. Two very different interpretations. Why? Because life experiences shape how we interpret things. If I had to guess, when the Leviticus 18 girl heard me say the church should love gay people, she assumed that I affirmed same-sex marriage; her mind was made up before I even opened the Bible to talk about traditional marriage. The guy who thought I was a homophobe has probably met Christians who believed in traditional marriage and *also* really did hate gay people. Maybe those people even looked like me and quoted the same verses I did.

The nature of belief is tricky. Rarely do we believe things simply because we took a levelheaded look at all the facts and dispassionately formed our beliefs from those facts. Instead, our beliefs are formed in a complex web of emotions, life experiences, stories, fears, and tribal allegiances.

One of my favorite scholars who talks about this phenomenon is Jonathan Haidt. Haidt is a renowned social psychologist who loves to study why people believe what they do. His book *The Righteous Mind* is one of my top five most important books I've read in the last ten years. The subtitle says it all: *Why Good People Are Divided by Politics and Religion*. Haidt isn't a Christian, and he doesn't talk about anything related to gay people in his book. But I've found the book to be one of the most valuable guides in helping us navigate volatile conversations about faith and sexuality.

Haidt's fundamental thesis is that our beliefs and moral convictions mostly come from intuition ("gut feelings") and not rational thinking. In other words:

> Moral intuitions arise automatically and almost instantaneously, long before moral reasoning has a chance to get started, and those first intuitions tend to drive our later reasoning. If you think that moral reasoning is something we do to figure out the truth, you'll be constantly frustrated by how foolish, biased, and illogical people become when they disagree with you.[1]

Intuition refers to our unconscious reasoning or our instincts: those gut-level feelings we get when we just *know* something is wrong. For instance, say you back your car up and slam into a dog, sending its soul to doggy heaven (or doggy hell, if it's my neighbor's yappy dog). Should you eat the dog? Most of you would probably say, "No, it's wrong to eat a dog!" And maybe you're right. But why? Is dog meat not tasty? Have you ever tried it? Is it not as nutritious as, say, pig? "Dogs are dirty," you might say. But you'll eat ham and hot dogs and McDonald's—or at least, you probably wouldn't say it's morally wrong for people to do so.

---

1. Jonathan Haidt, *The Righteous Mind: Why Good People Are Divided by Politics and Religion* (New York: Vintage Books, 2012), xx.

"But no one eats dogs; it's just wrong," you might say. Actually, people in many countries eat dogs. The sale and consumption of dog meat is legal in Switzerland, China, Nigeria, and many other countries. About five million dogs are slaughtered for meat every year in Vietnam. Killing dogs for meat has only been illegal in the US since 2018.

The fact is, for most of us, our aversion to eating dog meat comes from our intuition, not our rational reasoning. Few of us have sat down and waded through all the arguments for and against eating dog to come to a rational conclusion built on evidence that eating dog is morally wrong.

Haidt illustrates his point using the picture of an elephant and a rider. Our intuitions are like an elephant that's going to go where it wants to go; the rider represents our rational thinking, the part of us that analyzes arguments, considers evidence, and looks at the facts. The rider has little influence over the elephant. Instead, the rider's ability to "just go with the facts" or "follow the science" is hindered by the fact that they're sitting on an elephant of intuition. "People made moral judgments quickly and emotionally," writes Haidt. "Moral reasoning was mostly just a post hoc search for reasons to justify the judgments people had already made."[2]

As another example, you could imagine that our intuitions are the *president* of our beliefs, while our rational thinking acts as our press secretary—always defending and supporting our

---

2. Haidt, *Righteous Mind*, 47.

beliefs but rarely truly reevaluating them.[3] A press secretary can't be reasoned into going against the president's orders. In order to get people to change their minds, we must speak to their presidents—their intuitions. They need to *desire* a different sort of belief before they can rationally embrace it. If you want to convince someone to actually eat a dog, you'll have to do more than just give them a culinary lesson on the nutritiousness of Chihuahua.

Haidt's work confirmed so much of what I was experiencing in the conversation about same-sex sexuality.[4] Two Christians might be reading the same Bible, the same verses, even the same translation, and yet come to two very different conclusions about whether the Bible supports same-sex marriage. I can give a talk to one audience and be hailed as highly convincing, while another audience might disagree with almost everything. That's because every person listening is 90 percent elephant. "If you ask people to believe something that violates their intuitions, they will devote their efforts to finding an escape hatch—a reason to doubt your argument or conclusion. They will almost always succeed."[5]

Reading Haidt's work got me on a kick of reading other cognitive and social psychologists who say similar things about the nature of belief. Nobel Prize winner Daniel Kahneman

---

3. See Haidt, *Righteous Mind*, 90.

4. My friend Greg Coles has a great blog post that teases this out: "Your Arguments about Sexual Ethics Matter Less Than You Think," The Center for Faith, Sexuality & Gender, December 11, 2018, www.centerforfaith.com/blog/your-arguments-about-sexual-ethics-matter-less-than-you-think.

5. Haidt, *Righteous Mind*, 59.

writes about how the mind works in his highly acclaimed book *Thinking, Fast and Slow*, and psychologist Adam Grant applies similar principles in his book *Think Again*—a book about how to rethink your own beliefs and help others do the same.[6] These books and others, along with my anecdotal experience, have shown me that our beliefs are not the result of marinating our prefrontal cortexes in a bunch of facts. And this reality should reshape how we go about contentious conversations like the ones we're having in this book.

Does this mean rational arguments are irrelevant? I really hope not, because much of what follows in this book is rational argument! My point is that rational arguments *alone* rarely persuade if there's no appeal to a person's intuition. A well-reasoned argument is much more believable if it comes from a person whose posture is genuine, humble, and kind. A preachy preacher yelling from a stage will be less compelling than a preacher who knows your name. Or as the old adage goes, kids will rarely remember what their parents have said; what they'll remember is how their parents made them feel.

My intention in this book, then, is not to arm you with arguments so you can go pummel someone with your viewpoint and destroy theirs in the process. While I do give intellectual responses to intellectual arguments, I'm also wanting to embody

6. Daniel Kahneman, *Thinking, Fast and Slow* (New York: Farrar, Straus and Giroux, 2011); Adam Grant, *Think Again: The Power of Knowing What You Don't Know* (New York: Viking, 2021).

a kind of posture that I think is most conducive to fruitful conversations. Here are some overarching things you can do toward this end.

First, be willing to rethink your point of view. This is incredibly difficult—some might say risky—but it should be a no-brainer. I mean, if you're not willing to rethink your view, why would you expect someone else to rethink theirs? I love how Adam Grant illustrates this point by identifying four types of reasoners: preachers, prosecutors, politicians, and scientists. *Preachers* preach sermons at people to promote their view (in Grant's perspective, anyway), *prosecutors* recognize flaws in someone else's reasoning, and *politicians* simply want to win over their audience. But *scientists*—at least in theory—are in search of truth. "We move into science mode when we're searching for the truth: we run experiments to test hypotheses and discover knowledge."[7]

A real scientist is more interested in discovering truth than being right. They're eager to rethink what they believe if their belief is shown to be incorrect. Daniel Kahneman, who I mentioned above, is one of the smartest people on the planet. He recalls a time when he listened to a lecture where the speaker refuted something Kahneman had written about. Kahneman's reaction? *He was ecstatic!* "I've had my viewpoint corrected, so now I'm closer to the truth!"[8] This should be our goal, and this goal should saturate our posture. We want to be closer

---

7. Grant, *Think Again*, 20.

8. Daniel Kahneman, quoted in Grant, *Think Again*, 61–62.

to the truth. And we should view our dialogue partner as a companion in the journey. Rather than focusing on how we can prove them wrong, we should ask the question, Where might they be right?

Second, be a genuinely curious person. This goes hand in hand with the previous point. We should be genuinely curious about the other person *and their viewpoint* if we expect them to be curious about ours. This does *not* come easy for most of us, since we believe our viewpoint is right and everyone who disagrees is wrong. True curiosity amid disagreement is tough, I know. But being curious about another person's point of view—*genuinely curious*—is essential if we ever want that person to actually consider our point of view. Plus, if we're actually more concerned with the truth than we are with defending ourselves, we should be eager to consider other points of view.

Being curious about the other person is also essential for profitable conversations. "What's your story? What have you been through? What are your likes and dislikes? *Who are you?*" When people feel like you're genuinely curious about them as people, this can turn down the temperature on what could normally be a heated conversation. More than that, it's the Christian thing to do. Paul said it's the kindness of God that leads to repentance (Rom. 2:4). So if you really think someone should repent, how kind are you?

Third, be a good listener. What Adam Grant says is so true: "When we try to convince people to think again, our first instinct is usually to start talking. Yet the most effective way to help others open their minds is often to listen."[9] I can't tell you how often I've found this to be true in my own life. Listening is so disarming. But it must be genuine listening. Some people listen just so they can catch someone making a false claim—they're listening in order to *refute*, not to *understand* what the person is saying. People can sniff out this posture, and it almost always causes their defenses to go up. When this happens, a profitable conversation has just ended.

If you're not able to genuinely listen to another person's viewpoint, what makes you think they'll listen to yours?

Fourth, ask good, honest questions. Formulate genuine questions, not leading or interrogating ones. Asking genuine and curious questions enables us to have a good, clear, and honest understanding of the other person's viewpoint. If we don't understand their view, we run the risk of straw-manning their view by painting it in the worst possible light (or simply not representing it accurately). Straw-manning another person's view will not encourage them to sincerely consider what you have to say. "Most people immediately start with a straw man," writes Adam Grant, "poking holes in the weakest version of the other side's case." Instead, take a "steel man" approach where you try your best to understand and accurately represent the strongest part of their argument. "Asking people questions can motivate them to rethink their conclusions."[10]

---

9. Grant, *Think Again*, 151.
10. Grant, *Think Again*, 136–37.

When people know you're not trying to misrepresent them or paint their viewpoint in the worst possible light, it shows that you're an honest person who's more interested in the truth than in proving your point. And what a sweet, profitable conversation it can be when two people are honestly in search of truth.

Fifth, find some point of agreement. Telling someone that you agree with them on certain points can be disarming. It shows that you're not just defending your view and trying to destroy theirs at all costs. It shows that you're genuinely searching for the truth. Finding points of agreement with the other person could encourage them to consider things they might agree with in your point of view. "When we point out that there are areas where we agree and acknowledge that they have some valid points, we model confident humility and encourage them to follow suit."[11]

Again, finding points of agreement shows that you're more interested in discovering the truth than you are in simply winning an argument at all costs.

Sixth, understand the power of belonging. Both Jonathan Haidt and Adam Grant talk about this. Haidt calls it our "hive switch," in the sense of bees interacting with one another in a beehive.[12] We are hive-ish creatures whose beliefs are part of our tribal identity. Changing our beliefs can cost us our membership in our tribe. "When people hold prejudice toward a rival group," Adam Grant says, "they're often willing to do whatever

---

11. Grant, *Think Again*, 112.
12. Haidt, *Righteous Mind*, 256–84.

it takes to elevate their own group and undermine their rivals—even if it means doing harm or doing wrong."[13] I know this to be true, because I lived through 2020, when different political tribes fought tooth and nail over mask mandates, lockdown measures, the efficacy of vaccines, and who should be the next president of the United States.

Our beliefs are significantly influenced by the tribe we belong to, and simply recognizing their tribalistic nature can go a long way in helping us dialogue better. For instance, if you were trying to convince the guy next door that the army is the most important branch of the military, and he served in the marines for twenty-five years, do you think he'll be convinced by any logical argument you throw his way? Our tribal allegiances impair our ability to evaluate rational arguments.

Understanding the power of one's tribe also has relational implications: changing views often results in changing tribes. It's important to keep this in mind, especially in LGBTQ conversations.

Say, for instance, you're a Christian parent trying to convince your intelligent lesbian daughter, who affirms same-sex marriage, that your church's traditional position on marriage is correct. You're not just trying to persuade her toward a different intellectual position. You're not just asking her to consider a different individual path. Rather, you're essentially asking her to leave her community and join yours. You have to honestly ask

---

13. Grant, *Think Again*, 124.

yourself, What would that be like for her? Would it be worth it? Would she leave behind a strong community for an even better one? Would anyone in her new community love her, care for her, ask her questions, and take her out to lunch? And how would that go with her current community? What would they say? How would she feel about leaving them? Would she lose friends? Would she gain new ones? Would her new community (your church) accept her and love her as much as her current one? How do you know? Do you know her current community? Their names, where they work, their likes and dislikes? How are the other lesbians doing in your community? If you were in her shoes, would *you* want to change communities?

Your daughter's view on same-sex marriage is likely wrapped up in a web of communal relationships and identity.

The same goes for you as a parent: changing your theological view would likely come at a great cost. We're never simply dealing with the cumulative weight of one set of theological facts against another. Fruitful conversations recognize that we're dealing with whole people who crave belonging, and our viewpoint is a membership card to community and relationships.

Last, don't be overly confident. Don't be afraid to express some uncertainty in your beliefs. This is, of course, counterintuitive, but I think Adam Grant is right: "Communicating [your beliefs] with some uncertainty signals confident humility, invites curiosity, and leads to a more nuanced discussion."[14]

---

14. Grant, *Think Again*, 117.

Grant is not saying—and I'm not saying—that we should have no convictions or confidence. He's simply saying that our convictions should be tempered by honest humility. I mean, all our beliefs have some stone unturned, some argument unexamined or underexamined. Remember, 90 percent of our beliefs are held by intuition. Can we really say that our "gut feelings" are rock solid and not subject to error? Only Jesus can claim 100 percent certainty. And when we're 100 percent certain of 100 percent of our beliefs 100 percent of the time (I'm looking at you, Enneagram Eights), we come across not as more convincing but as more foolish. "Here's where I'm at right now." "Based on the things I've read and the people I've talked to, I believe this, but I'm open to another viewpoint." Statements like these—if genuinely meant—show that we're on an authentic quest for the truth and that we see the other person as a fellow traveler rather than a threat to ward off.

SECULAR PSYCHOBABBLE?

Some of you may be thinking, *All of this is just secular psychobabble. Real Christians should be bold and courageous; we should just preach the truth with conviction.*

This is absolutely true: we should be bold and courageous, and we're commanded to preach the truth with conviction (and love). Paul reminded us of this in several of his letters. But even Paul was strategic in how he spoke and wrote in order to communicate the truth more effectively. We see this throughout his letters, especially 1–2 Corinthians and Philemon. Paul often used rhetorical devices to help persuade people of the truth.

Take Philemon, for instance. Paul wants Philemon to release his runaway slave, Onesimus, and take him back as a brother in Christ. Paul could have appealed to his authority as an apostle and demanded that Philemon obey his orders. But instead, Paul downplays his authoritative status by calling himself "a prisoner of Christ" (vv. 1, 9), "an old man" (v. 9), and a "friend" of Philemon (v. 1).[15] In fact, Paul never refers to himself as an apostle in his letter to Philemon. Instead of wielding his authority, Paul appeals to Philemon "on the basis of love" (v. 9). Paul could have said, "Look, Philemon, I'm an apostle and you're not; you'd better take Onesimus back, or else!" And this might have seemed bold and courageous. But it might not have been very effective. Paul seems to consider it more compelling for Philemon to cultivate his own conviction to receive Onesimus back rather than be forced against his will to do so. Paul was speaking to Philemon's elephant.

So I'm not arguing against being bold and courageous. I'm only suggesting a more holistically Christian *manner* in which we boldly communicate and embody the truth. When people are given relational space to choose to believe something, they're *more* likely to actually believe it, as opposed to feeling like they're being forced into it. "We can rarely motivate someone else to

15. See Timothy A. Brookins, "'I Rather Appeal to *Auctoritas*': Roman Conceptualizations of Power and Paul's Appeal to Philemon," *Catholic Biblical Quarterly* 77, no. 2 (2015): 302–21.

change. We're better off helping them find their own motivation to change."[16]

LOOKING FORWARD

For the rest of the book, we're going to dive into a whole lot of Bible, theology, and rational arguments. But I don't want us to lose sight of what we talked about in this chapter. Examining the reasonableness of our beliefs is important; no one should believe something that lacks intellectual and theological credibility, and the rest of this book will test that credibility. But if we leave this chapter behind and focus on gaining ammunition to win the next argument, our beliefs won't be as compelling and we'll end up fostering unprofitable conversations.

Now, there's only so much of this I can do in a book. I can't see your eyes, and you can't see mine. I can't hear your words, and you'll only hear me speak! (Or write.) Book-form communication limits our ability to live out the stuff we just talked about. The one thing I'll try to do, though, is explore the historically Christian view of marriage in a written tone that reflects what we discussed above.

As I articulate the historically Christian view of marriage in the next chapter, I'll try to be as honest as I can, highlighting points I think are strong and admitting points I find to be weaker. This isn't because I don't think this view is the best

---

16. Grant, *Think Again*, 146.

reading of Scripture. Quite the opposite. The more I study the topic, the more compelling I find this view to be. It's *because* I find it to be true that I don't feel the need to overstate its case or try to disguise weak theological evidence. Honestly, when people feel the need to resort to dehumanizing slogans, or when they can't agree with a single aspect of the other person's point of view, I start to wonder if they're compensating for unexamined weaknesses in their own view.

THE HISTORICALLY CHRISTIAN VIEW OF MARRIAGE

The bulk of this book will address arguments in favor of same-sex marriage. But before responding to these arguments, we first need to lay out the historically Christian view of marriage—the very thing these arguments are trying to refute. You may hear this view referred to as the traditional view, the orthodox view, or even the biblical view of marriage. I'll stick to the terms *historically Christian view* or *traditional view*, though no description is perfect. Just to clarify, when I say "historically Christian" or "traditional," this does not at all mean I'm advocating for everything that historic or traditional Christianity has believed about men, women, marriage, and sex. Nor does it mean that Christians have historically affirmed every single aspect of what marriage is. My focus here is on marriage's essential nature (what marriage *is*) and purpose (what marriage is *for*) refracted against the question of whether same-sex unions can be considered marriages.

For clarity's sake, here's a concise definition of marriage and sexual relations that I'll seek to unpack in this chapter:

> *Marriage is a lifelong one-flesh covenant union between two sexually different persons (a male and a female) from different families, united with the purpose of telling God's story of faithfulness and creativity; and sexual relationships outside this covenant union are sin.*

Some Christians might word things slightly differently, but the historic Christian church, in all its diversity, would agree with the essential aspects of this definition. The most important thing for me, though, is that I find a good deal of scriptural and theological support for this definition. Here are five reasons why.

1. SEX DIFFERENCE IS AN INTRINSIC PART OF WHAT MARRIAGE *IS*

This is, to my mind, the most important reason I believe in the traditional view. Some people race to certain prohibition passages like Leviticus 18 or Romans 1 to show that same-sex sexual relationships are sin. But I think this approach is wrongheaded. The main question in our conversation is *not* "Does the Bible prohibit same-sex sexual relationships?" The main question is "What *is* marriage?"

To believe in same-sex marriage, you must understand marriage to be something like *a lifelong union between two consenting humans.* According to the traditional view, while marriage is much more than sex difference, it involves no less than sex difference. Simply put, *sex difference is an intrinsic part of what marriage is*. That is, sex difference is built into the very nature of what marriage *is*.

Say, for instance, a Martian landed on Earth and learned a little bit of English. He bumps into you in line at Starbucks while your spouse is parking the car. You and he get to chitchat a bit, and then your spouse joins you in line. "Who is this?" the Martian inquires.

"This is my spouse," you say. "We're married."

"*Married?* I'm not familiar with that word," he says. "What does it *mean?*"

What would you say to the Martian?

A person who holds to a traditional view of marriage would describe the meaning of marriage in a way that includes sex difference as part of their definition. "Marriage is when a human male and human female love each other and want to start a family together …" or something like that. Someone who affirms same-sex marriage, though, will talk about two humans—not necessarily a male and female—falling in love and committing to each other. Sex difference won't be part of what marriage *means*. They might say that most marriages are between a man and a woman. But male/female sex difference would not be part of the intrinsic meaning of what they believe marriage to be.

Alien encounters aside, what does the Bible say? Where does the traditional view get its definition of marriage from? The main texts are Genesis 1–2 and various New Testament passages that point back to this creation passage.

Genesis 1 describes several differences in creation: heaven and earth, evening and morning, land and sea, day and night, light and darkness. Instead of these differences creating chaos, God orchestrates them to sing together in harmony—beautiful differences playing off each other to proclaim the glory of their Creator. The creation of humanity at the climax of Genesis 1 also participates in this stunning display of unity amid difference; God creates humanity in his own image as sexually different creatures, male and female:

> God created mankind in his own image,
>
>   in the image of God he created them;
>
>   male and female he created them. (v. 27)

The creation of humanity as sexually different persons, "male and female," is woven into the fabric of God's diverse creation account. "Male and female" describes our biological sex, and our different sexes are defined by the respective roles that humans play in reproduction. This is why God commands the male and female to "be fruitful and multiply and fill the earth" (v. 28 ESV).[1] One of the purposes of biological sex differences is reproduction. Genesis 2 goes on to paint a more intimate picture of how the male and female will go about fulfilling this command. Naturally, sex differences are explored even further in Genesis 2.

---

1. For a more thorough explanation, see my *Embodied: Transgender Identities, the Church, and What the Bible Has to Say* (Colorado Springs: David C Cook, 2021), 65–67.

For instance, Genesis 2:18 and 20 describe Eve as a *suitable* helper" for Adam.[2] It's tough to pick up in English, but the Hebrew word for "suitable" (*kenegdo*) expresses both sameness and difference. *Kenegdo* is a combination of two Hebrew words: *ke*, which means "as," "like," or "similar," and *neged*, which means something like "opposite," "in front of," or "against." The combination of both words (*ke* + *neged* = *kenegdo*) captures Eve's similarity to Adam and her difference. Eve is similar to Adam since she's *human*, and she's different from Adam since she's ... what? What is the main thing about Eve that makes her different from Adam? The traditional view says it's her biological sex. Adam is male, while Eve is female. Both are equally human; both are differently sexed.

A few verses later, Adam and Eve join together in marriage, and the same similarity and difference expressed in *kenegdo* are teased out again:

> The man said,

> "This at last is bone of my bones
>   and flesh of my flesh;
> she shall be called Woman,
>   because she was taken out of Man."

---

2. By the way, the Hebrew word for "helper," *ezer*, does not imply that Eve is lesser than or inferior to Adam. *Ezer* is often used of God when he "helps" Israel, often in warfare (Ex. 18:4; Deut. 33:7, 26, 29; Ps. 20:2; 33:20)—certainly not a fitting description of someone who's inferior.

> *Therefore* a man shall leave his father and his
> mother and hold fast to his wife, and they shall
> become one flesh. (vv. 23–24 ESV)

Genesis 2:24 is the "John 3:16" of all marriage passages. It's often quoted throughout the New Testament (and in Judaism around the same time) to express the essential nature of what marriage is. But notice the word *therefore* at the beginning of Genesis 2:24. Bible professors often tell their students, "Whenever you see the word *therefore* in the Bible, you need to ask, What's that *therefore* there for?" The cheesy wordplay is onto something. The "therefore" (or "for this reason," as some translations have it) connects the logic of Genesis 2:23 with 2:24. Like the word *kenegdo*, Genesis 2:23 celebrates Eve's similarity and difference. She is "bone of my bones and flesh of my flesh," which describes her common humanity. She's also to "be called Woman, because she was taken out of Man." This is a statement about difference—sex difference.

"Taken out of Man" refers back to when Eve was created from Adam's "rib," as most translations put it (v. 22). But the Hebrew term here is *tselah*, and it never means "rib" in the Bible. It almost always refers to the side of a sacred piece of architecture, like the tabernacle or temple.[3] *Tselah* means "side," and the image

---

3. According to John Walton, *tselah* occurs about forty times in the Old Testament, and "outside of Genesis 2, with the exception of 2 Samuel 16:13 (referring to the other side of the hill), the word is only used architecturally in the tabernacle/temple passages (Ex. 25–38; 1 Kings 6–7; Ezek. 41)"; see John H. Walton, *The Lost World of Adam and Eve: Genesis 2–3 and the Human Origins Debate* (Downers Grove, IL: IVP Academic, 2015), 78.

here is of the man being split in half to form a woman. The word *therefore* in 2:24, then, takes the common humanity and sex difference of Adam and Eve and builds it into the very meaning of the one-flesh union. The two that become "one flesh" in 2:24 are specifically the male (Adam) and the female (Eve), who was taken from his side; the one-flesh union is like a reuniting of what was split apart.

This one-flesh union is the biblical way of talking about marriage. And Genesis 2 is not just describing Adam and Eve's marriage but announcing what God created marriage to be as an institution.

We see this from the shift in perspective from Genesis 2:23 to 2:24. In 2:23, Adam is speaking in the first person when he celebrates reuniting with the one taken from his side. But in 2:24, the narrator jumps in to give a paradigmatic description of what marriage *is*: "*Therefore* a man shall leave his father and his mother ..." (This narrator, by the way, is identified as God in Matthew 19, as we'll see below.) The wording of the narrator's statement suggests that God considers Adam and Eve's one-flesh union to be paradigmatic of all future marriage relationships.

In short, to form a one-flesh union according to the Creator's design, the two persons need to be both human *and* sexually different.

This is how Jesus seems to understand the passage as well (Matt. 19). For Jesus, male and female sex difference is part of what it means to form a one-flesh marriage union:

> "Haven't you read," he replied, "that at the begin-
> ning the Creator 'made them male and female'
> [quoting Gen. 1:27], and said, 'For this reason
> a man will leave his father and mother and be
> united to his wife, and the two will become one
> flesh'?" (Matt. 19:4–5, quoting Gen. 2:24)

According to Jesus' logic, the creation of humans as male and female in Genesis 1:27 is an essential part of the definition of marriage in Genesis 2:24: "the two" who "will become one flesh" are precisely the "male and female" cited in 1:27. Notice that Jesus quotes 2:24, but instead of connecting it to 2:23, he brings in 1:27—an even more explicit statement about sex difference: "The Creator 'made them *male* and *female*.'"

Jesus' use of Genesis here is particularly noteworthy. To respond to the Pharisees' question about divorce, Jesus takes us back to the very essence of marriage. He sees a lax view of divorce as a departure from the intrinsic nature of what marriage is, which has been etched into the created order (Gen. 1–2). For Jesus, the Genesis passage isn't just the beginning of a story that's subject to change; rather, it's the blueprint against which all other practices should be measured.[4]

---

4. Following Darrin W. Snyder Belousek, *Marriage, Scripture, and the Church: Theological Discernment on the Question of Same-Sex Union* (Grand Rapids, MI: Baker, 2021), 59–60. Ephesians 5:31 is another important New Testament passage that refers to Genesis 1–2 in the context of marriage. Here, Paul quotes Genesis 2:24 in a climactic moment in his theological discussion about marriage (Eph. 5:21–33).

So, the historically Christian view of marriage understands sex difference to be an intrinsic part of what marriage *is*.

The affirming view of same-sex marriage would need to provide a more compelling reading of Genesis 1–2, Matthew 19, and other relevant passages and show that sex difference is not an intrinsic part of what marriage is. Some attempts have been made, which we'll wrestle with in Conversations 1 and 2.

2. SAME-SEX SEXUAL RELATIONSHIPS ARE ALWAYS PROHIBITED

Same-sex sexual relationships are mentioned in at least five places in Scripture: Leviticus 18:22 and 20:13; Romans 1:26–27; 1 Corinthians 6:9; and 1 Timothy 1:9–10. In each case, they are prohibited. Before I tease this out, I want to make two observations.

First, each of these five passages is in a context where lots of other sins are listed—sins that are frequently committed by straight people. Incest, adultery, sex outside marriage—you name it. Greed, envy, murder, deceit, malice, gossip—they're right there in Romans 1. So are arrogance, slander, and being disobedient to your parents. The point of these passages is *not* to highlight the sins of gay people but to underscore the sins of *all people* so that *all people* can recognize their need for Jesus. Straight Christians should never wave these texts around as proof that gay people need to repent. We should humbly look at these texts like mirrors of conviction, not banners of condemnation for others to see.

Second, the interpretation and application of all five of these passages are disputed by some modern scholars. (For what it's worth, the meaning of pretty much every verse in the Bible is disputed by somebody somewhere.) There's a dispute about whether these passages are referring to *all* same-sex sexual relationships or only certain kinds. We'll address several of these interpretive issues throughout the rest of this book (see, among others, Conversations 4 and 5). But the point still stands; it's something that few people dispute. *Whenever* same-sex sexual relationships are mentioned in Scripture, they are always prohibited.[5]

This is noteworthy, since Scripture rarely speaks with a unanimous voice when it comes to ethical or theological points. Take divorce, for instance. If you were to ask, "What does the whole Bible say about divorce?" you'd get a complicated answer. Deuteronomy 24 is pretty lenient on divorce. Ezra 9–10

---

5. There was a time when people would point to David and Jonathan, Ruth and Naomi, or even the centurion and his servant in Matthew 8 as examples of positive same-sex sexual relationships, but these have long since failed to convince responsible readers. David does say that Jonathan's love was "more wonderful than that of women" (2 Sam. 1:26), but this doesn't mean their relationship was sexual, since the ancients didn't automatically equate "love" to "sex," unlike many modern westerners. Plus, David was married (to several women, actually), which would make Jonathan's alleged sexual relationship with David an adulterous one. So even if David and Jonathan did have some kind of secret affair, it would be condemned, not praised, by Scripture. Ruth was Naomi's daughter-in-law, and sex between in-laws is considered incest in Leviticus 18:15. Some say that the centurion was in a pederastic relationship with the slave boy whom Jesus healed (Matt. 8:5–13). Since Jesus healed him, he must have approved of the relationship—so the argument goes. Pederasty was an ancient practice where older men of high social standing would have a sexual relationship with a teenage boy of low social status. There's no evidence in the text, though, that the centurion was in a sexual relationship with his young slave. But even if he was, is this the kind of relationship Jesus would approve of? You can probably see why these examples are rarely used as arguments for the affirming view any longer.

commands divorce. Malachi 2 seems to say that God *hates* divorce. Jesus says that divorce is wrong in Mark 10:5–9, but in Matthew 5:31–32, he seems to say that it's not wrong if there's been sexual immorality. Paul adds more caveats in 1 Corinthians 7, where an unbeliever might leave their Christian spouse. And on and on it goes. The biblical teaching on divorce is complicated; there are tensions and diversity.

Same with women in church leadership. Does the Bible endorse women in pastoral leadership? Regardless of where you land on this question, if you're honest, you'll admit that the *other* view—that nasty, terrible, no-good, wrong view!—has a verse or two in its favor. Romans 16:7 seems to say that a woman named Junia was an apostle, and 1 Corinthians 11:5 assumes that women are prophesying in a local church context. But 1 Timothy 2:12 and 1 Corinthians 14:34–35 seem to say that women aren't allowed to teach or exercise authority over men. And so the debate rages on—a debate I have no interest in resolving here. The point is, there are isolated texts that, by themselves, seem to offer support for one position or the other.

Take almost any doctrine and you'll find some tension, some difference, some trajectory in Scripture. Election, end times, Sabbath keeping—you name it. There's a beautiful unity to Scripture, but there are also beautiful tensions. Some things are prohibited in the Old Testament but permitted in the New, and some things are permitted in the Old but prohibited in the New.

But not when it comes to same-sex sexual relations. There are no tensions, developments, or differences between the Old and

New Testaments. Whenever Scripture mentions them, they are always prohibited.

Someone could argue that this way of reading the Bible is simply the product of a modern, white, Western way of seeing things. But actually, this reading is most prevalent among ancient, nonwhite, non-Western interpreters of the Bible. This leads to the third reason I think the historically Christian view of marriage is the most compelling.

3. THE MULTIETHNIC GLOBAL CHURCH AFFIRMS THE HISTORICALLY CHRISTIAN VIEW

The multiethnic global church across all denominations has agreed that sex difference is an intrinsic part of marriage and that same-sex sexual relationships are sinful, since they can't be considered marriages.

Let me clarify that I'm not appealing to this tradition as some stand-alone argument, as if we should believe in the traditional view because, *dagnabbit, this is what we've always done believed!* If you google my name, you're unlikely to find people describing me as "a stalwart defender of traditional Christian views." This third point is more of a way to cross-check my first two points. It's a way to help us as individuals not read into the Bible what we think it says. One of the best ways to prevent your individual self from reading into the text what you *think* it says (or what you *want* it to say) is to go global. Listen to other Christians and scholars living in different parts of the world. Pay attention to how different denominations and cultures are reading the text. Learn from people of different ethnicities, traditions, geographical locations, and socioeconomic statuses. This doesn't mean that everyone else is right and you are wrong. It just means that healthy interpretations are ones that transcend race, sex, denomination, and socioeconomic status.

If, for instance, a bunch of mostly white, Western, wealthy Christians hold to one view of marriage, and the overwhelming majority of ethnically diverse Christians across the globe hold to another, this doesn't in itself mean that one group is right and the other is wrong. Maybe all the wealthy white people are reading Scripture correctly—who knows? The point is that ethnically and denominationally diverse contexts often help cross-check our biases and nudge us to read the text more sensitively.

Going back to our point: The global, multiethnic, multidenominational church has, for the last two thousand years, believed that sex difference is an intrinsic part of what marriage is and that same-sex sexual relationships are always sinful. And I'm casting the net very widely. Protestants, Catholics, Greek Orthodox, Russian Orthodox, Coptic Christians living in Egypt. Chinese Christians, African Christians, Indian Christians—wherever Christianity has existed. No matter their theological beliefs or denominational practices, they all have read Scripture as teaching that sex difference is an intrinsic part of marriage and that same-sex sexual relationships are always sinful.

We global Christians can hardly agree on anything. We don't agree on the meaning of justification by faith, the end times, the role of women in the church, the nature of baptism, whether divorce should ever be allowed, and whether God chose you or you chose him. We don't even agree on what books belong in the Bible! But two of the few things we have agreed on for the last two thousand years are: sex difference is part of what marriage is, and same-sex sexual relationships are always sinful.

Now, there have been diverse viewpoints *within* the framework of a traditional view of marriage. For instance, some of the earliest theologians had a more negative view of marriage itself (Tatian, Tertullian, Jerome) or believed that sex difference will be done away with in the resurrection (Clement of Alexandria, Origen, Gregory of Nyssa). Later on, though, most Christians viewed marriage more positively. Augustine wrote extensively on marriage and explored the theological significance of sex difference in marriage. Jovinian held to a very high view of marriage and did not think that celibacy earned you a higher status in God's kingdom. Bernard of Clairvaux believed that sex difference will remain in the resurrection (so did Augustine in his later years), even when there will be no procreation. Thomas Aquinas agreed with Bernard, as did other later theologians who wrote about marriage, like Martin Luther, John Calvin, and Karl Barth. Despite all these different nuances about marriage, one point was always agreed on: sex difference is an intrinsic part of marriage, even if some elevated singleness over marriage itself.[6]

---

6. See Christopher Roberts, *Creation and Covenant: The Significance of Sexual Difference in the Moral Theology of Marriage* (London: T&T Clark, 2008).

Some say that this is because the global church never imagined the possibility of two adults engaging in a same-sex union. But this assumption is not actually true. Same-sex sexual relationships of many kinds were known to Christians throughout history. Several early church leaders addressed a variety of same-sex sexual relationships, which shows that it was something that they were constantly dealing with. The council in Ancyra in Asia Minor (AD 314) talked about the level of penance one would have to undergo after engaging in same-sex behavior.[7] Such councils were convened to address issues that the church was going through, not simply to make judgments about the secular world around them. The same goes for the so-called Books of Order. These were manuals for church life that discussed actual issues facing the church. *Constitutions of the Holy Apostles* was one such manual (AD 375), and it not only felt the need to affirm that "difference of sexes was formed in Adam and Eve" but also went on to condemn same-sex sexual relationships.[8]

Later on, several church manuals called penitentials were written to instruct priests on how to handle the confessions of churchgoers. Several penitentials written between AD 500 and 900 instruct priests on how to respond to believers confessing all kinds of same-sex sexual sin, including a man having sex with a

---

7. Following S. Donald Fortson and Rollin G. Grams, *Unchanging Witness: The Consistent Christian Teaching on Homosexuality in Scripture and Tradition* (Nashville: B&H Publishing, 2016).

8. *Constitutions of the Holy Apostles* 6.3, cited in Fortson and Grams, *Unchanging Witness*, 41–42. It's interesting that pederasty is addressed not in this section but only later on in 7.2.

boy, sex between male adults, and sex between women. There were different levels of penance given depending on whether the person was a lay person, deacon, priest, or bishop—as well as whether the person habitually engaged in same-sex sex or was a one-time offender. By the eleventh century AD, same-sex sexual relationships became such an issue for the church in Europe that a monk named Damian wrote a whole book condemning the practice.[9]

I think it would be a bit of a stretch to assume that the historic church believed in male/female marriage simply because they didn't have any category for consensual same-sex sexual relationships. Their views on marriage and same-sex relations appear to be rooted in God's design for marriage and sexual expression.

Our next point might feel like a detour, but it's actually crucial for understanding the traditional view, and it'll play an important role in several arguments we'll wrestle with later on.

4. MARRIAGE AND SEX ARE NOT ESSENTIAL TO HUMAN FLOURISHING

Christianity has a rich tradition that celebrates marriage yet downplays its necessity for living a flourishing life.[10] Marriage

---

9. Peter Damian, *The Book of Gomorrah.*

10. See Steven Holmes, "Listening to the Past and Reflecting on the Present," in *Two Views on Homosexuality, the Bible, and the Church,* ed., Preston Sprinkle (Grand Rapids, MI: Zondervan, 2016), 168–69. Of course, not every branch of Christian tradition would agree with this. While celibacy and singleness were praised by most early Christian leaders, some more recent Protestant traditions, beginning with Martin Luther, started to look down on singleness and elevate—one might say idolize—marriage to the point of considering it a human necessity.

is highly celebrated in the Bible and is (obviously) foundational for human civilization. But nowhere in the New Testament does God promise believers a spouse that they sexually desire. In the New Testament, marriage is a possibility, not a promise—a particular vocation, not an absolute right.

Jesus himself was a single man of marital age, and this wasn't because he couldn't find the right woman or thought marriage was sinful. There's something profoundly theological and countercultural about Jesus' singleness. The New Testament describes Jesus as the one who fully and ultimately bears God's image (2 Cor. 4:4; Col. 1:15), the one who perfectly embodies the Genesis 1 vision for humanity. Though he's divine, he's also perfectly human—a perfectly complete human *as a single person*. Scripture elsewhere elevates singleness and puts it on par with marriage (Matt. 19:10–12). Paul even says that the one who "does not marry ... does better" (1 Cor. 7:38) and that the widow will be "happier if she stays as she is"—unmarried (v. 40).

Christians throughout history have taken the New Testament's emphasis on singleness seriously. Both Western and Eastern Christianity had a high view of singleness and applauded those who pursued it. The New Testament doesn't say that singleness is just drudgery to get through, like waiting in line for the latest ride at Disneyland. (Or simply going to Disneyland.) Singleness is a high calling for us all, unless God leads us into marriage.

The New Testament says that marriage is both beautiful and sacred yet not something that's essential for living a flourishing life. If a person goes through their entire earthly life without marrying and having sex with the person of their dreams, no promise of the gospel has been broken. Practically, of course, this might be very tough for some people. Many of us live in a highly sexualized culture that has convinced even Christians that true happiness is found in having sex and sex and more sex with people we think are sexy. And gasoline is thrown on the fire when more than 60 percent of us are doped up on porn. Add to this the idolatry of marriage that pervades the church, and we've created an environment where *not* marrying the person of your dreams could feel like a nightmare. Theologically, though, there's nothing in the rich and challenging call to follow Jesus—who happened to be a single man of marital age—that promises us a lovely spouse who will complete our humanity.

A robust understanding of Christian marriage includes the recognition that neither sex nor marriage is essential for human flourishing. We should be theologically suspicious of any argument—whether from conservatives or progressives—that implies that people can't really live a meaningful and flourishing life if they don't marry and have sex with a person they sexually desire.

5. MARRIAGE HAS A PURPOSE

This fifth and final defense of the historically Christian view is a bit more complex than the others and could take the rest of the book to unpack. It moves beyond the question "What *is* marriage?" and asks, "What is marriage *for*?" What's the purpose of marriage? Catholics, Protestants, and Orthodox Christians have wrestled with this question for millennia and haven't all landed on the exact same page, though there have been some broad points of agreement, which I'll highlight below.

I'll briefly sum up three purposes of marriage that I find to be most clearly revealed in Scripture and then consider these points against the backdrop of the possibility of same-sex marriage.

Symbolism

Marriage is the foundation stone upon which family and therefore society is built (see the next point below). And throughout Scripture, marriage is also used as an image to describe God's relationship with Israel (Isa. 50:1; 54:1–10; 62:4; Jer. 2–4; Ezek. 16; 23; Hos. 1–3) and Christ's relationship with the church (Matt. 22:1–14; 25:1–13; 2 Cor. 11:2; Eph. 5:22–33; Rev. 19–21). Paul goes so far as to say that human marriages are ultimately about Christ and the church:

> We are members of his body. "For this reason a man will leave his father and mother and be united to his wife, and the two will become one flesh." This is a profound mystery—but I am talking about Christ and the church. (Eph. 5:30–32)

The term *mystery* refers to something that was hidden in the past but is now revealed. I love how Christopher West (citing Pope John Paul II) puts it:

In creation, God's mystery of love "became a *visible reality through the union* of the first man and woman" (see Gen. 2:24). In redemption, that same mystery of divine love becomes "*a visible reality in the indissoluble union of Christ with the church.*"[11]

God wants to be one with us. He's given us his Spirit as a down payment of the ultimate and final unity he'll have with us (Eph. 1:13–14). And human marriage is one signpost pointing to that great and final moment when God will "bring unity to all things in heaven and on earth under Christ" (Eph. 1:10), when we will "participate in the divine nature" (2 Pet. 1:4) and celebrate "the wedding of the Lamb" (Rev. 19:7), when heaven and earth will become one. The one-flesh union formed by a man and a woman, therefore, tells God's story of creation and redemption.

Marriage also tells God's story of reconciliation, and it does so in such a way that sex difference plays a vital role. Here's what I mean. Marriage, as a one-flesh union, participates in and testifies to the overarching story of Scripture, where God seeks to reconcile and bring unity to things that are different. This theme is intrinsic to the bookends of Scripture, Genesis 1–2 and Revelation 21–22, and also surfaces at various other points in

---

11. Christopher West, *Our Bodies Tell God's Story: Discovering the Divine Plan for Love, Sex, and Gender* (Grand Rapids, MI: Brazos, 2020), 110, quoting John Paul II, *Man and Woman He Created Them: A Theology of the Body,* 2nd ed. (Boston: Pauline Books and Media, 2006), 97:4.

the biblical story line. Take Ephesians, for instance. Throughout this book, we see the theme of reconciliation between difference popping up all over the place. God is reconciled to humans (2:1–10), which brings reconciliation to different ethnic groups (2:11–22) and to people with different gifts (4:1–16), different familial relationships (6:1–4), and different social statuses (6:5–9). Paul's lengthy discussion of marriage in 5:22–33 participates in and reflects the broader creational pattern of reconciliation between differences. "What [Paul] says about husbands and wives in chapter 5 therefore comes within a larger context where in and through Jesus Christ the whole world is brought into a new unity."[12]

At the end of the Bible, heaven and earth are rejoined to each other and marriage is a symbol used to describe this coming together of creational differences into one (Rev. 19:7–9; 21:2, 9–10; 22:17). "The new Jerusalem is coming down from heaven like a bride adorned for her husband. This symbolism of marriage, of male and female coming together … tells us that here we find the very heart of God's intended creation."[13]

The coming together of male and female in a one-flesh marriage union tells God's story both of his relationship to humanity and of his desire to reconcile all the beautiful diversity of creation in unity to himself.

---

12. N. T. Wright, "From Genesis to Revelation: An Anglican Perspective," in *Not Just Good, but Beautiful: The Complementary Relationship between Man and Woman,* Helene Alvaré and Steven Lopez, eds. (Walden, NY: Plough, 2015), 92.

13. Wright, "From Genesis to Revelation," 89.

Could a same-sex union tell this same story? Some say yes, and we'll wrestle with their arguments in due time. One hurdle for the affirming view is how the phrase "one flesh" is used in key marriage passages. As we've seen in Genesis 1–2, Matthew 19, and other passages, sex difference seems to be a prerequisite for forming a one-flesh union. So when Paul cites Genesis 2:24 at the climactic moment of comparing marriage to Christ and the church in Ephesians 5, it seems like sex difference between husband and wife is an indispensable part of the story he's trying to tell.

In any case, my point here is not to wrestle with all the arguments and counterarguments. The main thing to keep in mind is this: any responsibly Christian understanding of marriage must show how it participates in God's overarching story of creation, redemption, and reconciliation. Simply relying on modern assumptions about romance, compatibility, and sexual desire as foundations for marriage is theologically unimpressive.

Procreation

Procreation is another purpose of marriage. Much of what makes males and females different has to do with the respective roles they play in conceiving children. As we saw above, the most fundamental statement about sex difference in Scripture (Gen. 1:27) is followed by the command to "be fruitful and multiply" (v. 28 ESV). Adam and Eve are commissioned to populate the earth, and their one-flesh union (2:23–24) is the means by which they carry out this creation mandate.

Procreative potential is not just a description of Adam and Eve's marriage in the garden; rather, it's a paradigm of God's design for marriage for all time. The birth and rearing of children are designed to take place within the lifelong covenant of marriage between a man and a woman.

Throughout both Testaments, having kids—or trying to have kids—was an intrinsic part of marriage. And this is true of virtually every society in human history. Even in societies where same-sex sexual relationships weren't deemed immoral, they still believed that marriage was, at least in part, *for* procreation.[14] The Old Testament takes this for granted and even institutes certain laws to safeguard marriages that happen to be infertile.[15] I used to think that the New Testament downplayed procreation in marriage. But after taking a closer look, I realized that it doesn't really downplay the procreative purpose of *marriage*; instead, it elevates *singleness* as a legitimate vocation for those who aren't called to have kids.

This doesn't mean that every marriage will result in procreation. A marriage can be open to procreation yet suffer from infertility. The same goes for couples who marry in old age, past the point of procreative probability. Due to advanced age, such marriages might not result in procreation apart from a miracle from God, but as male and female they still embody the structures of a procreative union and therefore testify to God's creative design.

14. See Stephanie Coontz, *Marriage, a History: From Obedience to Intimacy, or How Love Conquered Marriage* (New York: Viking, 2005).

15. Deuteronomy 25:5–10; cf. Genesis 38:8.

Chosen childless marriages—ones that aren't infertile but deliberately choose to prevent procreation from happening—are more disputed within the church. This might be the greatest challenge to procreation as a purpose of marriage. For most of church history, chosen childless marriages weren't considered to be in line with God's design for marriage. Marriage was for the creation of children, at least in part. But more recently in the Western Protestant church, it's not uncommon for marriages to deliberately prevent procreation. Is chosen childless marriage a valid option for male/female marriage, or is it going against God's intention for marriage? Christians who agree that marriage is between male and female disagree on how to respond to this question of chosen childlessness. And affirming Christians are quick to expose some inconsistent ways that traditional Christians understand marriage and procreation.

Personally, I lean more Catholic on this question. If a Christian couple came to me and said, "We feel called to get married, but we absolutely don't want to have kids," I'd say, "The theological burden of proof rests on you to show that you are actually called to marriage." I mean, I'd try to use a little more pastoral grace than that, but you get the point. I'm not ready to say that chosen childless marriages aren't real marriages or are always and everywhere going against God's design. There's some theological complexity here, and I don't think Scripture speaks with absolute clarity on this question. But on the whole, marriage has an intrinsic procreative structure or biological potential built into it, which testifies to God's own ability to create.

Humans bear God's image as male and female, and God's first command—to "be fruitful and multiply"—reflects his own creative ability. Inasmuch as sex difference is an intrinsic part of what marriage *is*, and procreation is therefore part of what marriage is *for*, it seems that those called to marriage are also called to try to have kids—if they truly are called to marriage and not just overwhelmed with romantic emotions.

I know this raises even more questions, but I want to get back to my main point. God created marriage to be the context in which kids are raised. A historically Christian marriage, then, will embody and be open to procreation, as it tells God's story of his life-giving creative power. This doesn't mean that every marriage *will* result in raising kids. What it does mean is that true marriages will reflect God's designated context in which kids should be raised.

Companionship

A final purpose of marriage is companionship. Throughout the Song of Songs, for instance, we see a man and woman enjoying each other's friendship and bodies. Other passages in Scripture depict married couples delighting in companionship, reflecting God's delight in his people. Marriage isn't viewed as some emotionless baby-making institution. It is designed, in part, to be a particularly intimate way humans bond with each other.

It's important to point out, though, that marriage is not the only—not even the primary—way in which humans can find companionship. While Genesis 2:18 ("It is not good for the man to be alone") is sometimes taken to mean that marriage is God's solution to loneliness, this reading is problematic for at least three reasons. First, Eve was not *just* Adam's spouse; she was also the second human created. She represents not just a spouse but also human community. "Man is 'alone' because he is the only bodily creature made in God's image and likeness," writes Christopher West.[16] Second, the creation of Eve was necessary to fulfill the creation mandate of Genesis 1:28 ("be fruitful and multiply" ESV). It wasn't good for Adam to be alone, *not* because he needed a spouse to solve his loneliness but because he couldn't fulfill the command he was given without a procreative partner. Third, throughout Scripture, nonsexual friendship is almost always described as fulfilling the human longing for companionship. Christopher Ash says it best:

> The Bible has a great deal to say about the longings of the human heart. This is more pronounced in some places than in others, but there is much about love, friendship and fellowship. It is very striking, however, that almost never are these longings and their satisfaction placed in the context of a sexual relationship.[17]

---

16. West, *Our Bodies Tell God's Story*, 31.

17. Christopher Ash, *Marriage: Sex in the Service of God* (Vancouver, BC: Regent College Publishing, 2005), 117. Ash surveys the following passages to prove his point: 1 Samuel 18–20; 2 Samuel 1:26; John 13–16; 1 Corinthians 13; 1 Thessalonians 2:6–8; 1 John 4:7–21.

The historically Christian view of marriage considers companionship to be one purpose of marriage alongside all others, but it doesn't consider marriage to be the only—or even the primary—way in which humans find love.

WRESTLING WITH THE PURPOSE OF MARRIAGE

These purposes of marriage have been discussed in various ways throughout church history. And while Orthodox, Catholic, and Protestant churches have tended to emphasize certain purposes of marriage over others, "all branches of Christian tradition share an ecumenical consensus on the creational-covenantal form of marriage: one man and one woman, joined in sexual-social unity, promised in exclusive-enduring fidelity."[18] The affirming view, of course, disagrees with the "one man and one woman" requirement, and the rest of this book will interact with the main reasons why. For now, it's important to recognize *that* marriage has a purpose (or purposes) that goes beyond simply romantic interest and compatibility.

Any compelling Christian theology of marriage should be able to offer biblically faithful responses to the questions, What *is* marriage, and what is marriage *for*? The first two purposes above are the most challenging for the possibility of same-sex marriage, while the third one—companionship—by itself doesn't seem to pose much of a problem; same-sex couples certainly enjoy each other's companionship.

---

18. Belousek, *Marriage, Scripture, and the Church*, 34–35.

SUMMARY

Of these five reasons I believe in the historically Christian view of marriage, none of them focuses on sexual orientation—being *attracted* to the same sex. There's nothing in the Bible that says gay people (that is, people who experience same-sex attraction) are violating God's plan for marriage and sexual expression simply by existing.[19] And there's nothing in a traditional sexual ethic that requires a person's sexual temptations to disappear after coming to Christ. The language we use in same-sex marriage conversations should reflect this. It's not a legitimate argument to say things like, "The traditional view of marriage demands that gay people stop being gay" (since *being* gay simply means being attracted to the same sex). It's also unhelpful to say things like, "The traditional view of marriage prevents gay people from getting married" (since the traditional view is based on biological sex difference, not sexual attraction) or "The traditional view just wants gay people to be lonely" (since marriage isn't the biblical solution to loneliness).

The key question that distinguishes the affirming view from the traditional view of marriage is this: Is sex difference an intrinsic part of what marriage *is*—and why or why not?

Now, really smart Christians have disagreed with the historically Christian view of marriage, or significant aspects of it. And that's what the rest of this book is all about—responding to these arguments. I'm going to follow the same format for responding to

---

19. Some modern evangelical Christians disagree with me here. For a lengthier analysis and defense of my view, see my *People to Be Loved: Why Homosexuality Is Not Just an Issue* (Grand Rapids, MI: Zondervan, 2015), 144–49.

each of these twenty-one arguments: First, I'll summarize the argument as concisely and accurately as I can (some will take more ink than others). I'll then highlight aspects of the argument that I find most compelling and helpful. And finally, I'll offer a more critical response to the argument, highlighting points of disagreement.

Before we dive in, though, I want to make one more point—a point that was hinted at earlier. Wherever you're at on the question of *human* marriage, Christians of all theological persuasions should agree—indeed, *need* to agree—that Jesus is far more delightful, beautiful, and necessary for human flourishing. Human marriages don't even come close to the dazzling delight of being united with Christ in the new creation. If traditionalists prove their view of human marriage to be true from Scripture, then great. But if they miss out on the far greater reward of living in and delighting in the presence and lordship of Jesus—if marriage brings them more happiness than Jesus does—then this is a great loss. Likewise, if affirming Christians find satisfaction and value in reassuring themselves that their same-sex relationship is biblically justified yet don't experience the vibrant and life-giving presence of Jesus in their lives, then they have missed the true meaning of marriage.

We should all agree that this book and the topic we're wrestling with is ultimately about a shadowy, hazy replica of the real thing—living in and savoring the presence of the triumphant King who sacrificed himself and was raised from the dead to open up the doors of eternal pleasure for the ones who crucified him.

SEX DIFFERENCE IS *DESCRIBED*, NOT *PRESCRIBED*, IN SCRIPTURE

SUMMARY

Genesis 1–2 does highlight sex difference when it talks about marriage. After all, humans had to populate the earth, grow the nation of Israel, and produce a lineage that would ultimately lead to the Messiah. And it's true—most people are heterosexual and will probably get married to the opposite sex. However, heterosexual marriages are *normal*, not *normative*. They may be *described* in Genesis 1–2, but they're not being *prescribed*. Just because the Bible contains opposite-sex marriages does not in itself mean they are the only kind of marriage blessed by God.

Some scholars go on to point out that Genesis 1–2 doesn't give us a comprehensive picture of the way things always must be; there are valid exceptions to the normative nature of Genesis 1–2. Take the existence of intersex persons. Most people are clearly male or female. But we know that some people are born with a Disorder/Difference of Sex Development (commonly known as intersex), and in some cases, they have both male and female sexual anatomy.[1] Likewise, just because land and sea are described in Genesis 1 doesn't erase the existence of other bodies of water like rivers and marshes and swamps. Similarly, just because Genesis 1–2 mentions male and female, who come together in a heterosexual union, doesn't mean that other types of marriage are forever ruled out. "Adam and Eve can be understood as the majority story rather than the exclusive model for what it means to be human," writes theologian Megan DeFranza. "By extension, heterosexual marriage can be seen as the majority story, not the exclusive model."[2]

POINTS OF AGREEMENT

This argument is valuable for at least a couple of reasons. First, it quickly challenges lazy statements like "Adam and Eve, not Adam and Steve." The fact that Adam and Eve were different sexes, and that they were the first married couple in Scripture, doesn't in itself mean that every person should follow their lead. Simply citing Genesis 1–2 isn't enough to establish a definition of Christian marriage.

---

1. For more on intersex, see my *Embodied: Transgender Identities, the Church, and What the Bible Has to Say* (Colorado Springs: David C Cook, 2021), 113–26.

2. Megan DeFranza, "Journeying from the Bible to Christian Ethics in Search of Common Ground," in *Two Views on Homosexuality, the Bible, and the Church,* ed. Preston Sprinkle (Grand Rapids, MI: Zondervan, 2016), 90.

Second, I love that this argument brings intersex people into the interpretation of Genesis 1. It's quite common for Christians to talk about male and female without even thinking about intersex persons. And it is certainly true that Genesis 1 does not give us a comprehensive description of creation. There exist lots of "in-betweens" that go unmentioned, such as swamps (neither land or sea), dusk (neither day or night), and amphibians (neither land or sea animals).

So is sex difference in marriage being *described* or *prescribed* in Genesis 1–2?

RESPONSE

For several reasons, I think the answer is both. Adam and Eve's sex difference is *described* but also *prescribed* as normative for all future marriages. Notice the shift in language from verse 23 to 24 in Genesis 2. We touched on this in Foundation 2, but it's worth looking at again.

In verse 23, Adam speaks as he celebrates the creation of his wife, but verse 24 shifts back to the voice of the narrator, who makes a more general statement about marriage. If all we had were 2:23, we could say that the passage is merely descriptive, not prescriptive. But 2:24 shifts from the particular context of Adam and Eve to make a normative statement: "This is why a man leaves his father and mother and bonds with his wife, and they become one flesh" (CSB). The author isn't just describing Adam and Eve at this point but is prescribing what marriage intrinsically *is*.

This is also how Jesus invokes the verse, as we saw in Foundation 2:

> Haven't you read ... that at the beginning the Creator "made them male and female" [Gen. 1:27], and said, "For this reason a man will leave his father and mother and be united to his wife, and the two will become one flesh" [Gen. 2:24]? (Matt. 19:4–5)

Jesus goes back to the creation story primarily to show that marriage is intended to be permanent. He also says the voice speaking in Genesis 2:24 is "the Creator," which imbues the Genesis text with prescriptive force. God's intention for marriage is permanence, and most scholars who affirm same-sex marriage agree that permanence is prescriptive rather than simply descriptive. It seems selective, then, to say that Jesus believes Genesis 1–2 *prescribes* permanence but only *describes* sex difference, when both are inherent to the texts he cites.

Some affirming scholars will agree that permanence is prescriptive but argue that neither Genesis nor Jesus is talking about sex difference. Affirming scholar Karen Keen says, "Loyal, covenanted love, *not sexual differentiation*, is the foundation of biblical marriage."[3] Affirming writer Matthew Vines says something

---

3. Karen R. Keen, *Scripture, Ethics, and the Possibility of Same-Sex Relationships* (Grand Rapids, MI: Eerdmans, 2018), 30 (emphasis mine). Keen is summarizing the progressive argument in this context and not necessarily endorsing it, but she doesn't later come back and revise this argument. Instead, she goes on to say, "Jesus reads Genesis

similar: "The Genesis text focuses only on what these two have in common. Adam and Eve's sameness, *not their gender difference*, is what makes them suitable partners."[4] But why can't the text have both sameness and difference in mind—both covenanted love and sexual differentiation? When Jesus cites Genesis 1:27 ("the Creator 'made them male and female'"), he affirms both human equality and sex difference. It seems like a false dichotomy to say that Jesus cites Genesis 1–2 to affirm permanence and equality but not sex difference, when Jesus explicitly names all three: permeance, equality, *and* sex difference. It's more reasonable to just say that Jesus believes everything he said.[5]

The intersex analogy described above is interesting to me, since a few of my friends are intersex. Some take the existence of intersex persons, which seems to fall outside the assumptions of Genesis 1–2 ("male and female he created them," 1:27), to be analogous to same-sex marriage, which also falls outside the pattern of marriage in Genesis 2. This argument then shows that Jesus affirms the eunuch in Matthew 19:12, and those who were born eunuchs were basically intersex—they had some atypical feature in their sexual anatomy. Since Jesus affirms eunuchs

1:27 as God creating human beings as a pair but his argument *does not focus on sexual differentiation*" (Keen, *Scripture*, 31 [emphasis mine]).

4. Matthew Vines, *God and the Gay Christian: The Biblical Case in Support of Same-Sex Relationships* (New York: Convergent, 2015), 49 (emphasis mine).

5. This doesn't mean that Jesus had same-sex couples in mind when he cited the passage and was reaching to Genesis 1–2 to argue against same-sex marriage. At the same time, sex difference is inextricably woven into Jesus' main point that marriage is between *two* people and it's to be permanent. The sex binary of male and female is inseparable from the main point Jesus is making, and so it doesn't seem like a compelling interpretation to say that Jesus believed the stuff about "two" but not the stuff about "male and female."

without trying to cram them into some male or female box, so also we could follow Jesus' logic and validate marriages that don't fit the heteronormative box.

It's an interesting analogy. Before we assess it, we should first say a few things about intersex persons.

Intersex is a broad umbrella term that describes at least twenty different medical conditions where a person is born with some atypical feature in their sexual anatomy and/or sex chromosomes. It's important to note that almost all people with an intersex condition (99 percent, according to some estimates) are clearly male or female.[6] Simply having an intersex condition doesn't mean you're neither male nor female, nor does it mean that intersex is evidence of a third sex. Even in some extremely rare cases where there is a significant blend of male and female sexual anatomy, this doesn't mean that there are other categories of biological sex in addition to male and female. Most people are clearly male or female, and some might appear to be both. But male and female are the only sex categories for *Homo sapiens* because, as a sexually dimorphic mammalian species, humans have only two kinds of gametes (sperm and egg). That's how we reproduce; there is no third gamete.

So where does this leave us with the eunuch (as intersex) and same-sex marriage? Does Jesus' praise of the eunuch provide any evidence that he might also affirm same-sex marriage?

The analogy faces at least two challenges.

---

6. See Leonard Sax, "How Common Is Intersex? A Response to Anne Fausto-Sterling," *Journal of Sex Research* 39, no. 3 (2002): 174–78.

First, Jesus brings up the eunuch as a symbol for singleness, not to expand his understanding of marriage. Eunuchs were for the most part infertile men and were almost never married. This is why Jesus mentions them; he brings them up in response to the statement, "It is better not to marry" (Matt. 19:10). The eunuch in Matthew 19 isn't offered as a way of expanding Jesus' previous statement about marriage. Quite the opposite. The eunuch shows that abstaining from marriage, which Jesus understands to be between male and female (vv. 4–5), is a valid and noble path.

Second, even if the (one born a) eunuch is a person with an intersex condition (and I think this is probably right), this still doesn't mean that they're left out of Genesis 1:27. The text technically says, "Male *and* female he created them." People with a severe intersex condition don't fall outside the language of this statement, since the text doesn't say *every single human will perfectly embody one of the two sex categories of male and female.* Again, male and female are the two sex categories that exist for all mammals, and this is true even if some intersex persons exist with both male and female sexual anatomy.[7]

While there are some helpful things that this argument asks us to consider, I don't think it provides a better reading of Genesis 1–2 and Matthew 19 than what the traditional view offers. Sex difference does seem to be etched into God's blueprint for marriage in Genesis 1–2, and Jesus appears to affirm this.

---

7. Another point to consider is the possibility that intersex conditions are part of the fall and therefore would not have existed in a Genesis 1–2 world. I address this in more detail in my book *Embodied*, 125–26.

"ONE FLESH" DOES NOT IMPLY SEX DIFFERENCE

SUMMARY

This argument is similar to the previous one. It seeks to show that Genesis 2 does not say that sex difference is part of marriage. To do so, it focuses on the meaning of "one flesh."

The argument proposes that "one flesh" in Genesis 2:24 refers to a new kinship bond regardless of sex difference. "The language of 'one flesh' in Genesis 2:24 does not refer to physical gender complementarity, but to the common bond of shared kinship," writes New Testament scholar James Brownson.[1] As with the previous argument, this one acknowledges that the majority of marital relations will probably be heterosexual. But such sex differences are not inherent in the phrase "one flesh."

Brownson is the main scholar who has championed this argument, but several others have more recently embraced it. In fact, if

---

1. James Brownson, *Bible, Gender, Sexuality: Reframing the Church's Debate on Same-Sex Relationships* (Grand Rapids, MI: Eerdmans, 2013), 35.

you must know, *I* actually embraced it back in 2015 in my book *People to Be Loved.*[2] Though I ended up embracing the traditional view of marriage in the book, when it came to the meaning of "one flesh" in Genesis 2, I was convinced of Brownson's argument. (I no longer am, as we'll see.)

POINTS OF AGREEMENT

What I loved about Brownson's argument (and still appreciate) is that he based his argument in the lexical meaning of the word "flesh" (*basar* in the Hebrew). This word by itself often refers to one's family or kinship. For instance, Laban said to his nephew Jacob, "You are my own flesh and blood" (Gen. 29:14). We see similar statements throughout the Old Testament (Judg. 9:2; 2 Sam. 5:1; 19:12–13; 1 Chron. 11:1). In all these texts, "flesh" refers to family, and sex difference is not intrinsic to the word's meaning.

Moreover, the Hebrew word *dabaq*, sometimes translated "cling" or "cleave," never refers to sexual union in the Old Testament. But it does refer to a kind of kinship bond in, for instance, Ruth 1:14, where Ruth "clung" to her mother-in-law, Naomi.[3]

---

2. See Preston Sprinkle, *People to Be Loved: Why Homosexuality Is Not Just an Issue* (Grand Rapids, MI: Zondervan, 2015), 29–31.
3. See Brownson, *Bible, Gender, Sexuality*, 88.

RESPONSE

As a Bible nerd who loves a good word study, I was impressed by Brownson's work on the word *flesh*. It does indeed most often refer to a person's kin, not to their sexual partner of the opposite sex. Something I didn't pay close attention to in my previous agreement with Brownson is the unique phrase *"one* flesh." Laban didn't say to Jacob, "We are *one* flesh," but "You are my own flesh and blood." There's a difference between "flesh," which is used all over the place in the Bible, and "one flesh," which is quite rare. In fact, the only time "one flesh" occurs in the Bible is in Genesis 2:24 and its later citations (Matt. 19:5–6; Mark 10:8; 1 Cor. 6:16; Eph. 5:31). All these occurrences of "one flesh" are describing a sexual relationship between two sexually different persons. Matthew 19 is particularly clear:

> "Haven't you read," he replied, "that at the begin-
> ning the Creator 'made them *male* and *female*
> [quoting Gen. 1:27], and said, 'For this reason
> a man will leave his father and mother and be
> united to his wife, and *the two* will become *one
> flesh*'?" (Matt. 19:4–5, quoting Gen. 2:24)

Linguistically and logically, "the two" that "become *one flesh*" are the "male and female" of the previous statement. How does Brownson get around this? Well, to be honest, he doesn't really deal with it. He simply says that Jesus sees in "Genesis

2:24 a vision for the permanence of marriage."[4] But why can't it be both? Clearly, Jesus is concerned about permanence—"What God has joined together, let no one separate" (Matt. 19:6). But does this mean he can't also believe what the verse says about sex difference? To my mind, there's no compelling reason why Jesus doesn't believe what he said about *both* permanence and sex difference.

The same goes for the original context of Genesis 2. Brownson says that the focus of Genesis 2:21–25 "is not on the *complementarity* of the man and the woman but on the *similarity* between the two."[5] To support this, he cites the first half of 2:23, where Adam cries out, "This is now bone of my bones and flesh of my flesh." But Brownson leaves out the rest of the verse, which says, "She shall be called 'woman,' for she was taken out of man."[6] As we saw in Foundation 2, the first half of 2:23 highlights Eve's *similarity*, which Brownson mentions, and the last half of the verse highlights Eve's *difference*—sex difference—which Brownson doesn't mention. Neither does Brownson deal with the word *kenegdo* (vv. 18, 20), which also underscores Eve's similarity to *and difference* from Adam.

"One flesh" also occurs in Paul's quotation of Genesis 2:24 in Ephesians 5:31. Brownson says that "one flesh" conveys the idea of faithfulness between the married couple and that while

---

4. Brownson, *Bible, Gender, Sexuality*, 94.

5. Brownson, *Bible, Gender, Sexuality*, 86.

6. He does the same thing on page 106—citing the first half of Genesis 2:23 but not the second half.

Paul has in mind a husband and wife, sex difference isn't necessary for spouses to be faithful to each other.[7] This isn't a bad
point. One could argue that male/female marriage was the only
kind of marriage available to Paul, so of course he'd address
husbands and wives when talking about marriage. One problem
with this reading, though, is that the meaning of "one flesh" is
rooted in the creation narrative, where sex difference is built into
the phrase. Paul's understanding of sex difference in marriage
is not just culturally normal but theologically normative. That
is, Paul's *theology* of marriage is dependent on how Genesis 1–2
inscribes marriage into creation, making it unlikely that Paul
simply assumed that marriage is between a man and a woman
because that's just the way they did it back then.

What makes better sense of Paul's actual point, then, is that
"one flesh" implies both fidelity and *unity amid difference*—the
latter being a pervasive theme in Paul's letter to the Ephesians
(e.g., 2:11–22; 3:8–12; 4:1–16).

Paul also refers to the one-flesh union in 1 Corinthians 6:16,
where he rebukes a Corinthian man for having sex with a prostitute: "Do you not know that he who is joined to a prostitute
becomes one body with her? For, as it is written, 'The two will
become one flesh'" (ESV). It would seem odd to say that this man
has formed a new kinship bond with the prostitute. There's not
a lot of leaving and cleaving going on in a brothel. Brownson
recognizes this and says, "Sex with a prostitute is a parody and

---

7. Brownson, *Bible, Gender, Sexuality*, 97–101.

distortion of the true one-flesh union, and is thus to be avoided."[8]
I think Brownson might be right here. Sex with a prostitute is a
"parody" of "the true one-flesh union" (i.e., marriage), in that
they are acting as if they were married even though they are
not. But Brownson's interpretation of 1 Corinthians 6:16 doesn't
really support his view about same-sex marriage. Everywhere else
in Scripture, "the true one-flesh union" is a marriage between
male and female. So, inasmuch as Paul's quote from Genesis 2:24
in 1 Corinthians 6:16 honors the original context of Genesis 2, it
seems more likely he's using the phrase "one flesh" to describe a
sexual relationship between male and female.

Brownson's not troubled by this, however. "The fact that
the Bible uses the language of 'one flesh' to refer to male/female
unions *normally* does not inherently, and of itself, indicate that it
views such linkages *normatively*."[9] But as I stated in the previous
argument, this kind of reasoning doesn't make the best sense of
the text. The normative shape of Genesis 2:24, along with how
Jesus interprets the passage in Matthew 19, suggests that "one
flesh" does indeed describe a *normative* union between two sexually different persons.

In sum, I agree that the "one flesh" statement in both Genesis
and the New Testament describes a new kinship bond, but it's a
false dichotomy to say that it's therefore *not* a bond between two
sexually different persons. Scriptures seems to say it's both.

---

8. Brownson, *Bible, Gender, Sexuality*, 101.
9. Brownson, *Bible, Gender, Sexuality*, 105.

NO ONE ACTUALLY BELIEVES IN "BIBLICAL MARRIAGE"

SUMMARY

"'Biblical Marriage,'" writes affirming scholar Megan DeFranza, "was heterosexual, but it was also patriarchal, often uniting an adult man to a child or teenage girl with little education and fewer legal rights."[1] The Bible is filled with all kinds of marriages that no modern Christian should endorse. Men marry females captured in war (Deut. 21:10–14), take concubines as wives to bear children if their original wife was infertile (Gen. 16:1–2), and, in one disturbing case, kidnap virgins and take them home as wives (Judg. 21). Or they simply take another wife if they can afford it; or two, or three, or four—seven hundred in the case of Solomon (1 Kings 11:3). Women are told to marry their rapist (Deut. 22:28–29) and are treated as little more than property in

---

1. Megan DeFranza, "Journeying from the Bible to Christian Ethics in Search of Common Ground," in *Two Views on Homosexuality, the Bible, and the Church*, ed. Preston Sprinkle (Grand Rapids, MI: Zondervan, 2016), 89.

some cases, existing solely to serve their husbands (Deut. 21:14). "Contemporary Christian marriage is not 'biblical marriage' of the Old or New Testament," says DeFranza.[2]

POINTS OF AGREEMENT

This argument is a great response to anyone who flippantly throws around the phrase "biblical marriage" to refer to male/female marriage while ignoring all the aberrant kinds of marriages that no Christian should endorse today. Anyone who is a genuinely curious reader of the Bible should be troubled by some (many?) marriages in the Old Testament, which is one reason I don't prefer the phrase "biblical marriage."

RESPONSE

This argument raises some good points, but it also suffers from several problems. Most importantly, it confuses the *is* with the *ought*. In other words, just because something is depicted in Scripture doesn't mean God thinks we ought to do that. Take the marriage by kidnapping in Judges 21. The tribe of Benjamin was nearly destroyed through a civil war, many of the remaining men didn't have wives, and no other tribe wanted to give their virgin daughters to them in marriage. So what does Israel do? They orchestrate a plan where all the single Benjamite men could

---

2. DeFranza, "Journeying from the Bible," 90.

go and each kidnap a fresh virgin and take her home. The whole scene is a great big mess.

But that's the point. The entire book of Judges is a great big moral mess. Things go from bad to worse to downright horrific as Israel spirals down into moral chaos. The six major judges who rise up to rule part of Israel keep getting morally worse and worse, ending with Samson—who, contrary to popular opinion, is *not* a morally upright character (Judg. 13–16). After Samson dies, the book concludes with a sort of appendix (Judg. 17–21) that paints one of the darkest pictures of humanity in the Bible. As far as marriage goes, the end of Judges gives us the *is* (it tells us *what* happened), but it doesn't give us the *ought* (how we *should* behave). If there's any "oughtness" built into the story, it goes like this: for everything that's good and holy, please do not live this way. And the same goes for much of the Bible after Genesis 3.

The Bible is a complex book filled with many different genres, literary devices, purposes, and themes. And the authors of the Bible are honest storytellers who aren't afraid to describe how evil humans can be. The Bible's mention of Solomon's seven hundred wives, for instance, shows that he failed as a king (1 Kings 11:1–6). "The king ... must not take many wives," says Deuteronomy 17:16–17. Solomon's *is* directly violated God's *ought*.

When reading the Bible, then, we have to ask the question, Is this kind of human behavior being *encouraged* or simply *described*? Some statements are straightforward to interpret. "You shall not commit adultery" (Ex. 20:14) pretty much means you shouldn't have sex with another person's spouse. Other passages, especially narratives, are a bit trickier. When Simeon and Levi found out that a guy named Shechem had raped their sister, Dinah, they killed every male and looted the city (Gen. 34). Was this righteous revenge or an unjust display of excessive violence? The narrator doesn't make it crystal clear (though Gen. 49:5 suggests the latter).

Just because the Old Testament talks about morally twisted kinds of marriages doesn't mean we should go and do likewise.

But what do we do with the marriages that *do* seem to be commanded? Sometimes it seems that God himself is totally fine with, for instance, a woman marrying her rapist. Check out Deuteronomy 22:

> If a man happens to meet a virgin who is not pledged to be married and rapes [*tamas*] her and they are discovered, he shall pay her father fifty shekels of silver. He must marry the young woman, for he has violated her. He can never divorce her as long as he lives. (vv. 28–29)

The first thing to notice is that this passage is what's called a case law, not an apodictic law. Don't worry if you don't know what *apodictic* means. I didn't either until I was halfway through my PhD. Basically, apodictic laws are direct moral imperatives from God, the "thou shalt" and "thou shalt not" kinds of commands in the Bible (the Ten Commandments, for example). Case laws have to do with specific situations that might arise in a particular culture; they have an "if/then" character to them. If your neighbor's cow falls into your ditch, then here's what you are to do. That's case law. And that's the kind of law being described here in Deuteronomy 22. It's situational, contextual, and tethered to a particular time and place.

The second thing to notice is that this passage is probably talking not about rape but about something more like seduction—a man wooing a woman into sleeping with him. The word translated "rape" here is *tamas*, a word that doesn't typically refer to "rape." Although there isn't a verb in Hebrew that specifically means "rape," verbs of violence are utilized by the biblical authors to communicate force. Hebrew *hazaq*, "to sieze," is one of those—for example, in 2 Samuel 13:11 when Tamar is raped by her brother. In fact, just a few verses earlier, in Deuteronomy 22, we do see an actual rape situation where *hazaq* is used, but the woman is deemed innocent because she was forced, while the man who perpetrated the crime is guilty of rape—*hazaq*, not *tamas*—and is given the death penalty (v. 25)! "Do nothing to the woman," the text goes on to say; "she has committed no sin deserving death" (v. 26). When rape is clearly in view, the woman is not commanded to marry her rapist.

Compare this with an ancient Mesopotamian law, which says not only that the female victim of rape *should* marry her rapist but also that the wife of the rapist is to be raped and then sold into slave-concubinage.[3] Women are tossed around to and

---

3. Middle Assyrian Laws A §55; see Sandra L. Richter, "Rape in Israel's World ... and Ours: A Study of Deuteronomy 22:23–29," *Journal of the Evangelical Theology Society* 64 (2021): 59–76.

fro like shekels in a busy market. Laws about rape, seduction, and marriage in Deuteronomy 22 are actually much more humane than what we find in the surrounding culture.

I'm not at all saying that everything in this passage is good and beautiful and should be integrated into Christian marriage manuals. Again, this is case law, not apodictic law. As a modern Christian, I still find this passage to be disturbing. All I'm saying—and what many Old Testament scholars are saying—is that, in its own historical and cultural context, this law was an improvement on the ways in which women were treated in ancient times.

Plus, even though certain laws in the Old Testament were an improvement on those of the surrounding cultures, they still weren't ideal. That is, not every old covenant law perfectly reflected God's original intention. Jesus makes this exact point when the Pharisees question him about divorce. "Is it lawful for a man to divorce his wife for any and every reason?" the Pharisees ask (Matt. 19:3). The Pharisees then rightly cite Deuteronomy 24, where Moses commanded "that a man give his wife a certificate of divorce and send her away" (Matt. 19:7). They seem to have the Bible on their side. But Jesus gives them a lesson in biblical interpretation: just because it's in Old Testament law doesn't mean it reflects God's original creation design. "At the beginning," Jesus says, "the Creator 'made them male and female,'" joining them together in a one-flesh union—a union that God joined together; therefore, "let no one separate" (vv. 4–6).

For Jesus (and the New Testament writers), there is something distinct about the ethical and theological place Genesis 1–2 has in the canon of Scripture. Even if the laws of Deuteronomy and Leviticus improve on their surrounding environment, they still fall short of the original creational vision: "In the image of God he created them; *male and female* he created them" (Gen. 1:27). Genesis 1–2 is a blueprint for how things *should* be—the *ought*, not just the *is*. Things fall apart after Genesis 3, but the rest of Scripture reveals a God who's slowly bringing us back to the way things were meant to be.

To come full circle, then, when people use the phrase "biblical marriage," they don't always mean that *everything contained in the Bible about marriage is good and beautiful and holy*. At least, I hope they don't. "Biblical marriage" should mean something more nuanced and carefully attuned to the shape of the biblical story and the role Genesis 1–2 plays in Christian ethics.

PAUL WAS NOT TALKING ABOUT CONSENSUAL SAME-SEX RELATIONSHIPS

SUMMARY

According to this argument, the five prohibition passages (Lev. 18:22; 20:13; Rom. 1:26–27; 1 Cor. 6:9; 1 Tim. 1:9–10) are not talking about consensual same-sex relationships between equals. Rather, they prohibit sexual exploitation, abuse, or other forms of nonconsensual relationships (rape, pederasty, prostitution, master/slave, etc.). Or they address certain kinds of same-sex sexual relationships where one partner had a much higher social status than the person he was having sex with; power differentials were built into ancient same-sex relationships. Consensual same-sex relationships between equals didn't exist back then, so Paul and others couldn't have been addressing consensual relationships.

POINTS OF AGREEMENT

I'll never forget first coming across this argument and getting defensive: "This can't be true ... They're just reading into the text what they want to see!" But then I stepped back and spent a good deal of time looking at the background literature in Greek and Roman sources, and I was blown away. Text after text, I saw male same-sex relationships being described by ancient authors in ways that were not consensual. Older men having sex with teenage boys (a practice known as pederasty), masters having their way with their male slaves, and many other kinds of relationships where the active sexual partner was penetrating a passive partner of a lower social standing.

The fact is, in the Roman world (when the New Testament was written), male same-sex sexual relationships often existed within power differentials, and I have no doubt that when Paul and others thought about male same-sex sexual relationships, images of abuse and exploitation were immediately in view.

The main question, then, is this: Are the biblical prohibition passages referring *only* to abusive kinds of same-sex sexual relationships between unequals? To answer this question, I want to look at three things: (1) the language of the prohibition passages, (2) the background material, and (3) the nature of ancient literature. Please note: We will have to go fairly deep into some scholarly discussions to give this argument the honor it's due.

RESPONSE

First, the actual language of the prohibition passages does not seem to support this argument. Take Romans 1:26–27, for instance:

> Because of this, God gave them over to shameful lusts. Even their women exchanged natural sexual relations for unnatural ones. In the same way the men also abandoned natural relations with women and were inflamed with lust for one another. Men committed shameful acts with other men, and received in themselves the due penalty for their error.

Notice that Paul uses generic terms for men and women here: "Women exchanged ... Men also abandoned ... Men committed shameful acts with other men." In Greek literature, when active/passive power differentials are described, the words *erastēs* and *erōmenos* are often used to describe the dominant and dominated partner respectively. But Paul doesn't use these terms. Neither does he use one of the many Greek terms used to describe pederastic relationships, such as *paiderastēs* ("lover of boys") or *paidophthoros* ("corruptor of boys"). Slaves and slave masters aren't mentioned either. And neither are prostitutes. If Paul was primarily concerned about the age, social inequality, or lack of consent between the partners, he doesn't make this clear. The fact that he uses generic terms for men and women suggests that he doesn't have a particular kind of abusive relationship in view.

Also, Paul uses language of mutuality to describe the relationship: "inflamed with lust *for one another* ... committed shameful acts *with other men* ... received *in themselves* the due penalty for *their error.*" Such language wouldn't make sense if Paul was thinking only of an abuser and an abused person. It's unlikely that Paul would condemn the victim of abuse—a teenage boy, for instance, whose parents gave him up to sexually please a wealthy older man. It does seem that Paul's language applies to consensual same-sex sexual relationships.

Moreover, Paul mentions female same-sex sexual relationships and compares them to male same-sex relationships: "Their women exchanged ... *In the same way* the men also abandoned ..." Now, some think that Paul's not even talking about female relations here. Instead, he's referring to nonprocreative heterosexual sex acts, like anal sex. This opens up a whole new set of questions, which we'll deal with in Conversation 7.

For now, let's assume, with most scholars, that female same-sex sexual relations are in view. What does this tell us about the kinds of relationships that Paul has in view? More specifically, what kinds of *female* same-sex sexual relationships were common in Paul's day? Some assume that Paul had no category for adult, consensual same-sex sexual relationships, but the historical evidence suggests otherwise, especially with women.

For instance, the third-century BC Greek poet Asclepiades references two women, Bitto and Nannion, who engage in sexual relations with each other. We don't know any other details, but the language suggests that they are both adults and engaging in consensual sex.[1] Erotic love between women was depicted quite frequently on vases and other works of art. One scholar, in fact, says that "representations of female-female human couples far outnumber female-male couples in prehistoric art."[2] While vase paintings from the Greek era typically show heterosexual couples or male pederastic scenes, we see several examples of women engaging in homoerotic behavior. And as far as we can tell, most if not all of them are between adult women of the same age and status.[3]

There are several references to same-sex female sexual relations around the time of the New Testament. And these relationships are sometimes described with marital language or depicted as marriage-like. For instance, the Christian author Clement of Alexandria mentions that "women behave like men in that women, contrary to nature, are given in marriage

---

1. "The Samian girls Bitto and Nannion are not of a mind / To meet with Aphrodite on her own terms / But desert to other practices, and not good ones [a reference to same-sex sexual love]" (Asclepiades, *AP* 5.207). Scholar Bernadette Brooten says that a later commentator "added as an explanatory note that Asklepiades was accusing them of being *tribades*"—a term used to describe female same-sex relations; see Brooten, *Love Between Women: Early Christian Responses to Female Homoeroticism* (Chicago: University of Chicago Press, 1998), 42.

2. Brooten, *Love Between Women*, 57n126 summarizing the work of Gabriele Meixner, *Frauenpaare in kulturgeschichtlichen Zeugnissen* (Munich: Frauenoffensive, 1994).

3. One of the most famous examples is a funeral relief dating back to around 6 BC that depicts two women holding hands in what's called the *dextrarum iunctio*, or "joining right hands," which often signified a marriage or marriage-like relationship.

[*gamoumenai*] and marry [*gamousai*] other women."[4] A second-century astrologer, Ptolemy of Alexandria (no relation to Clement), mentions women who take other women as their "lawful wives."[5] Iamblichos wrote a novel that describes an Egyptian queen, Berenike, who falls in love with and marries a woman named Mesopotamia.[6] Lucian of Samosata describes two women, Megilla and Demonassa, cohabitating by using terms related to marriage (Greek: *syneinai*, which was used in marriage contracts). He says that Megilla "married" (*gameo*) Demonassa and that Demonassa took Megilla as "my wife" (*emē gynē*).[7]

We could go on and list more references, but the point isn't really disputed. Female same-sex sexual relations were most often between two consenting adults. If these are what Paul has in view in Romans 1:26, then his language can't be limited to nonconsensual relationships. And again, Paul correlates these female same-sex relationships with male relationships in 1:27 ("In the same way the men also abandoned ...").

Male same-sex sexual relationships, on the other hand, were mostly between two social unequals—the active and passive partners—and were often nonconsensual. But we do have some examples of sexual relationships that seem to be more mutual and between social equals. For instance, there are many examples of same-age male youths engaging in same-sex

4. Clement of Alexandria, *Paidagogos* 3.3.21.3.
5. Ptolemy, *Tetrabiblos* 3.14.
6. See Photios, *Bibliotheke* 94.77a–b.
7. Lucian, *Dialogues of the Courtesans* 5.

relations, both from literary sources and, especially, from vase paintings.[8] In fact, same-age same-sex activity depicted on vases is so extensive that one expert in the field says that such scenes, along with other nonpederastic scenes between men, "may constitute as much as one third of all the homoerotic depictions extant on red figure vases."[9]

Several novels that date back to the first and second centuries depict male same-sex sexual relationships as between two consenting equals. Some might be tempted to dismiss this, since the examples are in novels, which aren't real. But in ancient novels, the line between fiction and nonfiction was blurry. Historians are quick to point out that such novels were designed to offer a commentary on real life—the way it is, or at least the way the author wants it to be.[10]

Xenophon of Ephesus's second-century AD novel, *An Ephesian Tale*, depicts a young man named Hippothous who falls in love with another man of the same age named Hyperanthes. Hippothous says, "Our first steps in lovemaking were kisses and caresses, while I shed floods of tears.... We were both the same age, and no one was suspicious. For a long time we were together,

---

8. See Theognis, *Elegies* 1063–64; Pindar, *Pythian* 10.57–60; Meleager, *AP* 12.109.1; see further Thomas K. Hubbard, "Peer Homosexuality," in *A Companion to Greek and Roman Sexualities*, ed. Thomas K. Hubbard (Oxford: Blackwell, 2014), 128–30.

9. See Hubbard, "Peer Homosexuality," 128–49 (130).

10. Classicist Kyle Harper shows that so-called fictional "literature is capable of expressing, in a way more intimate than mere commands, the shape of sexual morality when actually projected onto the furrowed plane of human life. Pagans, Christians, and Jews alike used stories as vehicles to express their deepest beliefs about the relationships between the sexual body, the mechanics of society, and the nature of the cosmos" (*From Shame to Sin: The Christian Transformation of Sexual Morality in Late Antiquity* [Cambridge, MA: Harvard University Press, 2013], 16; cf. 193, 236).

passionately in love."[11] Another novel by Achilles Tatius written around the same time depicts male lovers who are roughly the same age.[12] And the first-century novel *The Satyricon* appears to sanction consensual same-sex love between two of its main characters, Encolpius and Ascyltos: two adult men of the same social standing. This consensual relationship between equals "is not derided or labelled inappropriate," writes historian Laura Dunn,[13] which may be shocking, since most male same-sex sexual relationships were between two unequals. However, Dunn's entire thesis shows that the sexual norms and practices in ancient Rome were starting to change in the first century (when the New Testament was written). The cultural disdain for male same-sex sexual relationships between equals was starting to wane, which might be why Paul's language in Romans 1 doesn't appear to be limited to nonconsensual relationships.

In short, it would be historically inaccurate to say that Paul *must* be thinking of nonconsensual relationships since these were the only ones he could have known about when he wrote Romans 1.[14]

---

11. Xenophon of Ephesus, *Ephesian Tale* 3.2.

12. See Achilles Tatius, *Leucippe and Clitophon* 1.7–8, 12–14; 2.33–38. The relationship is pederastic, but both lovers are roughly the same age; see Robin Scroggs, *The New Testament and Homosexuality: Contextual Background for Contemporary Debate* (Philadelphia: Fortress, 1983), 134.

13. Laura A. Dunn, "The Evolution of Imperial Roman Attitudes toward Same-Sex Acts" (PhD diss., Miami University, 1998), 99.

14. Affirming writer Matthew Vines has critiqued some of the examples I cite in this section (https://reformationproject.org/same-sex-marriage-homosexuality-biblical-world). I've written a lengthy blog post responding to his critiques: "Did Consensual Same-Sex Sexual Relationships Exist in Biblical Times? A Response to Matthew Vines," The Center for Faith, Sexuality & Gender, August 30, 2022, www.centerforfaith.com /blog/did-consensual-same-sex-sexual-relationships-exist-in-biblical-times-a-response -to-matthew.

But all this background material is tainted by one important factor: elitism. This is our third point to consider—the nature of ancient literature.

Most of what we know about the Greco-Roman world, including its sexual practices and beliefs, comes from Greco-Roman literature. But who wrote this literature? For the most part, men did. And not just any men. Literate men (obviously). Since only about 10 percent of the population was literate during this time, the perspective we're given comes from this 10 percent. We have little access to the lives of the 90 percent *from the perspective* of the 90 percent. And most of the men who penned the literature weren't just literate; they were socially and economically elite men sequestered in wealthy urban centers of the empire, where they had little to no real contact with the large majority of common people.

Our window into the Greco-Roman world is a foggy one, clouded by the perspectives of wealthy, elite, literate men living in social compounds walled off from the rest of society.

Methodologically, then, relying on Greco-Roman literature to tell us everything we need to know about all the types of same-sex sexual relationships that existed at that time is quite problematic. It's like asking Donald Trump to tell us what life is like for an African American single mom living in Alaska. No doubt, Trump would have something to say. I'm just not sure it would be the most reliable description.

The same goes for our conversation. The argument that adult consensual same-sex relations didn't exist in Greco-Roman times relies on the perspective of a few wealthy, elite, literate men to tell us everything we need to know about the sexual practices and desires of common people, who weren't nestled at the top of the social pyramid. The literature simply doesn't give us an unbiased, comprehensive picture of life—all of life—on the ground. We don't know, firsthand, whether any slaves fell in love with other slaves of the same sex or whether a poor shopkeeper in Italy had a secret Brokeback Vesuvius affair with his male coworker. None of these lower-class people left behind personal testimonies of their actual lives. Maybe none of them had consensual same-sex sexual relationships, or maybe they did. We just don't know. The closest testimony we have from someone who rubbed shoulders with people of all social classes, not just the elite—who *was* literate and whose writings we have access to—is the apostle Paul.

Paul was a Roman citizen, which gave him a moderately high social standing. However, as a blue-collar worker (a tentmaker) and a Jew, he didn't possess the same high status as most other Greco-Roman authors. Most of all, he lived life in proximity to people of all social statuses, and he wrote in common language (Koine Greek) to common people. Paul gives us a unique window into the beliefs and practices of real people wrestling with their faith and sexuality.

On three occasions, Paul mentions same-sex sexual relations (Rom. 1:26–27; 1 Cor. 6:9; 1 Tim. 1:9–10), and on every occasion, he prohibits them. The language he uses contains no clear references to pederasty, abuse, or nonconsensual relationships. Even if we take the ancient background literature at face value, we can't historically say that Paul couldn't have known about consensual same-sex sexual relationships and therefore couldn't be prohibiting them. The evidence just isn't there. Paul's language is perhaps a better reflection of the actual practices and struggles of early converts living in the Roman world.

In short, there's nothing in the language of the prohibitions that limits them to nonconsensual relationships. It would be historically inaccurate to assume that Paul and others couldn't have known about consensual same-sex sexual relationships.

ROMANS 1 IS CONDEMNING EXCESSIVE LUST, NOT SAME-SEX LOVE

SUMMARY

Whereas the previous argument (Conversation 4) focuses on the *types* of same-sex relations, this argument focuses on the *reasons* men were having sex with other males. Both arguments try to distinguish between ancient forms of same-sex relations that were familiar to the biblical writers and current forms of same-sex relations that are characterized by romance, mutuality, and self-giving love—all the things that straight Christians strive to pursue in their romantic relationships.

Paul says in Romans 1:24–27 that "God gave them up in the *lusts of their hearts* to *impurity*, to the *dishonoring of their bodies*" and "to *dishonorable passions*." Men were "*consumed with passion* for one another" and committed "*shameless acts* with men" (ESV). James Brownson argues, "What Paul has in mind here is not the modern concept of homosexual orientation, that is, the notion that some people are not sexually attracted to those of the opposite sex at all, but instead are inclined to love those of the same sex." Paul and other ancient writers believed that same-sex sexual relationships were "a particular manifestation of self-centered lust, one that is not content with women alone but is driven to ever more exotic and unnatural forms of stimulation in the pursuit of pleasure."[1]

In other words, this argument proposes that Paul had a problem not with same-sex sexual relationships as such but with the excessive lust that led people to those relationships. Again, Paul had no category for same-sex orientation or same-sex couples who love each other without lusting after each other.

POINTS OF AGREEMENT

For a while, I considered this to be the strongest argument for affirming same-sex sexual relationships. I remember coming across this argument years ago, and I was taken aback. I hadn't heard of this argument before, and I was a little frustrated that I was never told about it in my evangelical environment. I kept seeing Christians simply quoting Romans 1, blissfully unaware of this argument (or other counterarguments), as if affirming Christians had never read Romans 1. Every affirming gay Christian I know is well aware of what Romans 1 *says*. They could

---

1. James Brownson, *Bible, Gender, Sexuality: Reframing the Church's Debate on Same-Sex Relationships* (Grand Rapids, MI: Eerdmans, 2013), 155–56.

quote it backward and forward, in Greek, Latin, and Coptic. They've been beaten over the head with it so many times that it's been etched into their psyche. This is why many affirming gay Christians have spent a good deal of time researching the actual *meaning* of Romans 1, and some have concluded that Paul is condemning excessive lust, not consensual love between people of the same sex.

This argument still doesn't say anything about sex difference in marriage, so even if it were true, the affirming view couldn't stand on this argument alone. But the argument does offer an interesting counterargument to the traditional interpretation of Romans 1. In fact, I spent a few months digging into the excessive-lust argument, because I initially found it to be challenging. I thought to myself, *If I can't refute this argument, then maybe it's correct.* So I cracked open my lexicon and other Greco-Roman sources to try to understand what Paul was saying in his own context.

Probably the strongest evidence in favor of this interpretation comes from ancient Greek and Latin writings. Many writers believed that same-sex sexual behavior was the result of excessive lust. For instance, the Ephesian Greek physician Soranus believed that the behavior of men who seek to be penetrated by other men "does not arise naturally in humans; rather, when modesty has been suppressed, it is lust that coerces to obscene usage body parts that have their own specific function, although there is no limit to desire."[2] Likewise, Dio Chrysostom says that those who pursue homoerotic

---

2. Soranus, *On Chronic Disorders* 4.9.131.

acts "seek another greater and more illicit form of outrage once they had become in every way sated and full of their unrestrained pleasure with women."[3] And Plato says that "the pleasure enjoyed by males with males and females with females seems to be beyond nature and the boldness of those who first engaged in this practice seems to have arisen out of an inability to control pleasure."[4]

So is Paul basically saying the same thing as these ancient writers? Does Paul condemn same-sex sexual relations because he thought they were the result of excessive lust? And would Paul have been perfectly fine with same-sex sexual behavior that wasn't driven by excessive lust?

RESPONSE

After living in this argument for a few months, I began to see some problems with the evidence used to support it.[5] Here are some points that caused me to question the excessive-lust view.

First, the background literature is way more diverse than what Brownson and others believe. It's easy to find some texts that talk about the excessive-lust lens; I quoted three above. But we also find many other perspectives in the literature. Plutarch's *Dialogue on Love*, in fact, says that *opposite-sex* sexual relationships

---

3. Dio Chrysostom, *Discourse* 7.149.

4. Plato, *Laws* 636.

5. I ended up producing a peer-reviewed theological article summing up my response to this argument; see Preston M. Sprinkle, "Paul and Homosexual Behavior: A Critical Evaluation of the Excessive-Lust Interpretation of Romans 1:26–27," *Bulletin for Biblical Research* 25, no. 4 (2015): 497–517.

are the result of excessive lust and that man-boy love is the only pure kind of sexual relationship: "There is only one genuine Love, the love of boys."[6] Because heterosexual sex "is so vigorous and powerful that it becomes *torrential* and almost *out of control*, it is a mistake to give the name Love to it."[7]

Diversity. That's the name of the game. Same-sex relations in the ancient world were way too diverse to assume that Paul considered them all to be the result of excessive lust. Thomas Hubbard, a classicist and world-renowned expert on homosexuality in the ancient world, sums it up best: "It is often assumed that same-gender relationships followed a stereotypical pattern and set of protocols in ancient society.... The texts, however, reveal a much wider diversity."[8] Some texts fit the excessive-lust model, but others do not. Brownson's assertion that "whenever same-sex eroticism is viewed negatively ... it represents the pinnacle of wanton self-indulgence at the expense of others" is overstated and, to be honest, simply untrue.[9]

Given the diversity of viewpoints in Paul's world, this leaves us to consider his actual words in Romans 1. What does *Paul* mean by what he said?

---

6. Plutarch, *Dialogue on Love* 4.

7. Plutarch, *Dialogue on Love* 4.

8. Thomas K. Hubbard, ed., *Homosexuality in Greece and Rome: A Sourcebook of Basic Documents* (Berkeley: University of California Press, 2003), 4–5.

9. Brownson, *Bible, Gender, and Sexuality*, 156. Negative references to same-sex sexual relationships that aren't focused on excessive lust are plentiful; for a small sampling, see Josephus, *Against Apion* 2.199; *Pseudo-Phocylides* 192; Philo, *Laws* 3.37–42; Martial, *Epigrams* 1.24, 12.42; along with virtually every text that condemns female same-sex sexual relationships.

When we look at Paul's words, we're quickly reminded that Paul speaks negatively about female same-sex sexual relations (1:26) and correlates them with male ones ("In the same way the men also ..." 1:27). Similar to what we saw in the previous conversation, female same-sex relations were described quite differently from male ones in Paul's day. And they weren't usually described as the result of excessive lust.[10]

In terms of Paul's language, he uses three different terms that are taken to be proof for the excessive-lust view: *epithumia* ("desires," 1:24), *pathos* (translated as "lusts" by the NIV in 1:26), and *orexis* (also translated as "lust" by the NIV in 1:27).

The first one, *epithumia* (1:24), simply means "desire" and can refer to a positive or negative emotion. Here, it's clearly negative, but we know this from the rest of verse 24—desires were directed toward "impurity" and "dishonoring of their bodies."[11] Plus, this verse is speaking not strictly about same-sex sexual relationships but about all forms of dishonorable (probably sexual) uses of the body.

The next word, *pathos* (1:26), is like *epithumia* in that it can refer to a positive or negative emotion. Here, it's clearly negative because it's modified by the word "dishonorable" (*atimia*)—God

---

10. The one exception might be Seneca, *Moral Epistles* 95.21, which condemns some women who indulge in drinking binges and "penetrate men" (figure that one out). In the context, though, Seneca critiques the women for acting like men. He never says that female homoerotic behavior is wrong because it is the product of excessive lust. Some Roman satirists also play on the manliness of some women, like Philaenis who "buggers boys," "bangs eleven girls a day," and lifts heavy weights "with an easy arm" (Martial, *Epigrams* 7.67). Not only is the historicity of such satirical pieces difficult to establish, but the point again is that some women acted like men in the bed and in the gym.

11. Scripture quotations in this paragraph and the next are taken from the ESV.

gave them over to "dishonorable passions" (*pathē atimias*). But remember, this phrase is describing *female* same-sex sexual relations. It's unlikely that Paul is critiquing them because they were the by-product of excessive lust. That's not what he says. He says their passions were dishonorable but not excessive.

The third word, *orexis* (1:27), is used only this one time in the New Testament, so it's a little more difficult to understand. It's used outside the New Testament to refer to sexual passion, lust, or a strong sexual desire. If any word is a candidate to support the excessive-lust argument, it's this one. But even *orexis* doesn't imply something that's intrinsically evil. A sexual act that is deemed to be pure could also be described with *orexis*. Sex does involve radical emotions and passions; sometimes they feel overwhelming. God doesn't say this is wrong, if expressed in a relationship he deems holy.

So does Paul speak negatively about same-sex sexual relationships because he believes they are the result of excessive lust? I used to think the text could be understood this way, but after I looked deeper into the diverse historical context and the actual meaning of Paul's words, this argument doesn't seem as convincing as it once was to me. And honestly? I thought it was a little fishy when James Brownson tried to capture Paul's point by saying, "It is not desire itself that Paul opposes, but excessive desire, which directs itself toward what is not rightly ours, overcoming self-control and obedience to God."[12] I mean, maybe. But that's not what

---

12. Brownson, *Bible, Gender, Sexuality*, 164.

Paul actually says. Again, Brownson describes Paul as condemn-ing *"self-seeking* desire," *"excessive* desire," "desire" expressed "in *increasingly extreme* and *destructive* ways," "desire that is *out of control*," "human desire in its *extremity*," and *"self-seeking lust* that *demeans* the other and *advances one's own agenda*."[13]

Self-seeking desire? Demeans the other? Advances one's own agenda? Do you see any of this in Romans 1? All these things certainly sound bad, but I can't help but think that Brownson is choosing terms to force Paul's actual words in the direction that he wants them to go. From my vantage point, "desire" (*epithumia*) and "passion" (*pathos, orexis*) are considered wrong in Romans 1 not because such desires are excessive—Paul never says they are excessive—but because they are satisfied in a sexual relationship that's deemed contrary to God's will.[14] It's the action, not the magnitude of desire itself, that Paul considers to be "contrary to nature" (v. 26 ESV).

The excessive-lust argument raises some good points and has forced me to go back to the text to see if I have understood Romans 1 correctly. Anytime an argument does that, it's a good day at the office. But after reflecting on all the evidence, I don't

---

13. Brownson, *Bible, Gender, Sexuality*, 160, 161, 164, 166 (emphases mine).

14. Both words, in fact, can have either a neutral or positive sense. Paul "with great desire" (*epithumia*) longed to see the Thessalonians face to face (1 Thess. 2:17 ESV; cf. Phil. 1:23), and Jesus "earnestly desired" (*epithumia*) to eat the Passover meal with his disciples (Luke 22:15 ESV). Both of these desires are good in light of the object of the desire. But when men and women desire to have sex with people of the same sex, and that desire leads to action—for it is the action that Paul critiques in Romans 1:26–27—it then becomes clear why *epithumia* and *pathos* are contrary to God's will here in this context. The cognate Greek verb *epithumeo* is also used in a positive or neutral sense: Matthew 13:17; Luke 15:16; 17:22; 22:15; 1 Timothy 3:1; Hebrews 6:11; 1 Peter 1:12.

think the excessive-lust view captures what Paul is actually saying in Romans 1. It's unlikely that Paul would be against same-sex sexual relationships that result from excessive lust while being perfectly fine with ones that don't.

THE BIBLICAL WRITERS DIDN'T KNOW ABOUT SEXUAL ORIENTATION

SUMMARY

According to the American Psychological Association (APA),

> Sexual orientation refers to an enduring pattern of emotional, romantic and/or sexual attractions to men, women or both sexes. Sexual orientation also refers to a person's sense of identity based on those attractions, related behaviors and membership in a community of others who share those attractions.[1]

The APA goes on to say that "sexual orientation ranges along a continuum, from exclusive attraction to the other sex to exclusive attraction to the same sex."[2]

---

1. "Sexual Orientation & Homosexuality," American Psychological Association, 2008, www.apa.org/topics/lgbtq/orientation.

2. "Sexual Orientation," American Psychological Association.

This argument says that ancient biblical writers were unaware that some people are innately attracted to the same sex. If they had known this, then they probably wouldn't have spoken negatively about same-sex sexual relations. "The reason why Paul argued as he did is that he ... believed that all people were heterosexual," writes Bill Loader, an affirming scholar.[3] Megan DeFranza likewise says, "If Paul were confronted with same-sex attracted Christians unable to change their orientation, I do not believe that he would respond with the same words we find in Romans, 1 Corinthians, and 1 Timothy."[4]

POINTS OF AGREEMENT

This argument highlights at least one solid point: our modern understanding of same-sex orientation is more advanced than what we find in ancient literature. Many in-depth studies have been done on sexual orientation, and some scholars have devoted their entire careers to understanding it. As modern interpreters of an ancient text, we should always be cautious about reading the

---

3. William Loader, "The Bible and Homosexuality," in *Two Views on Homosexuality, the Bible, and the Church,* ed. Preston Sprinkle, (Grand Rapids, MI: Zondervan, 2016), 45.

4. Megan DeFranza, "Journeying from the Bible to Christian Ethics in Search of Common Ground," in *Two Views*, ed. Sprinkle, 53. See also James Brownson, *Bible, Gender, Sexuality: Reframing the Church's Debate on Same-Sex Relationships* (Grand Rapids, MI: Eerdmans, 2013), 166, 170: "Writers in the first century, including Paul, did not look at same-sex eroticism with the understanding of sexual orientation that is commonplace today" and "the notion of sexual orientation was absent." Another affirming Christian, Matthew Vines, says that "same-sex relations in the first century were not thought to be the expression of an exclusive sexual orientation" (*God and the Gay Christian: The Biblical Case in Support of Same-Sex Relationships* [New York: Convergent, 2015], 106; cf. 23–44).

Bible through a modern, Western, post-Enlightenment lens. And a plain reading of the Bible shows that it doesn't talk about sexual orientation—at least in its modern form. It talks about sexual behavior and even sexual desire. But it doesn't specifically talk about the exact thing we now call same-sex sexual orientation.

RESPONSE

As I've considered this argument, two concerns come to mind.

First, I think it's overstating the case to say that "the notion of sexual orientation was absent" in the ancient world, as James Brownson says.[5] Some ancient writers did talk about an innate and seemingly fixed desire for the same sex that some people are born with. They didn't call it "sexual orientation," but the characteristics of what they *were* describing do seem to overlap quite a bit with our modern concept.

Aristotle said that some same-sex desires come from habit but others spring from nature.[6] This isn't exactly a quote from the APA, but the mention of nature is interesting. Another ancient writer believed that some men desire to play the passive role in same-sex intercourse because of a biological defect.[7] His theory is absurd and medically invalid. But the point is, he believed

---

5. Brownson, *Bible, Gender, Sexuality*, 170.

6. See Aristotle, *Eth.* 1148b, discussed in Martti Nissinen, *Homoeroticism in the Biblical World*, trans. Kirsi Stjerna (Minneapolis: Fortress, 1998), 81.

7. He says that semen is excreted into the anus, creating a need for friction (Pseudo-Aristotle, *Problemata* 4.26; cf. 879a36–880a5, 879b28–30).

that a particular form of same-sex erotic desire was *biological* and *inborn*.[8]

Parmenides, an early-fifth-century BC philosopher, believed that men who desired to be penetrated were "generated in the act of conception."[9] Likewise, a Greek physician from Ephesus named Soranus, who lived around the same time as Paul, believed that homoerotic desires were shaped more by nature than nurture. That is, men didn't just freely choose to have sex with men but were driven to do so from an internal desire.[10]

Again, I'm not saying these authors believed in the same thing that we call same-sex orientation. But there is at least some overlap, some semblance of our modern concept. Sexual behavior is described as the by-product of an innate desire.

The one scholar who's probably done the most work on this question is Bernadette Brooten. In her book *Love Between Women*, Brooten shows that some ancient writers believed that same-sex desires were fixed at birth. She gets this from looking at various medical, astrological, and magical texts. We'll see why these sources are important in a second.

One text says, "If the Sun and Moon are in masculine signs and Venus is also in a masculine sign in a woman's chart, women will be born who take on a man's character and desire intercourse

---

8. I'm not, of course, saying that the desire to be penetrated is the same as same-sex orientation.

9. Soranus, *On Chronic Disorders* 4.9.134, citing Parmenides, *On Nature* 5.15. See the translation and notes in Thomas K. Hubbard, ed., *Homosexuality in Greece and Rome: A Sourcebook of Basic Documents* (Berkeley: University of California Press, 2003), 464.

10. See Soranus, *On Chronic Disorders* 4.9.131–32, 134.

with women like men."[11] Another text written around the time of Paul says that if the sun and moon are at a particular location when a woman is born, she "will be a Lesbian, desirous of women, and if the native is a male, he will be desirous of males."[12] After looking at many more examples, Brooten concludes, "Contrary to the view that the idea of sexual orientation did not develop until the nineteenth century, the astrological sources demonstrate the existence in the Roman world of the concept of a lifelong erotic orientation."[13] And many scholars agree with Brooten.[14]

The sources of these examples are important for this reason: astrological and magical texts were very popular among common

---

11. Maternus, *Matheseos* libri viii 7.25.1. This work ("Eight Books of the Mathesis") dates to AD 334; see Bernadette J. Brooten, *Love Between Women: Early Christian Responses to Female Homoeroticism* (Chicago: University of Chicago Press, 1996), 132–37.

12. *Carmen Astrologicum* 2.7.6. See Brooten, *Love Between Women*, 119–20. The text has been preserved in Arabic. The word "Lesbian" translates the Arabic *sahaqa*.

13. Brooten, *Love Between Women*, 140.

14. See, among others, Amy Richlin, "Not before Homosexuality: The Materiality of the Cinaedus and the Roman Law against Love between Men," *Journal of the History of Sexuality* 3, no. 4 (1993): 523–73; Rabun Taylor, "Two Pathic Subcultures in Ancient Rome," *Journal of the History of Sexuality* 7, no. 3 (1997): 319–71. David Halperin has looked at many of these texts and argued that it would be wrong to find in them some ancient form of sexual identity (see his *One Hundred Years of Homosexuality: And Other Essays on Greek Love* [New York: Rutledge, 1990], 3–40). And Halperin is right: we can't use these texts to show that homosexuality as a sexual identity existed as such back then. The Greco-Roman world didn't have the same category of what we call "homosexuality" or "gay/lesbian" as a sexual identity. Ancient writers thought in terms of masculinity and femininity, and being masculine, for instance, didn't depend on whom you liked to have sex with. (Masculine men could have sex with women, boys, girls, or men; all that mattered was whether they were the active partner.) However, this doesn't change the narrow point I'm making. I'm not saying that we should read into the ancient material some modern idea of "homosexuality" as a sexual identity. What I am saying is that ancient writers did speculate about inborn same-sex sexual desires. People who had these desires weren't called "gay"; such an identity didn't exist back then. But I don't think this really matters. What matters is that they believed in an ancient form of an inborn, and sometimes fixed, desire to have sex with people of the same gender.

people. They were like an ancient version of the tabloid magazines you're forced to look at in checkout lines.[15] It's not like these statements were tucked away in some ivory-tower textbook read only by elites. The assumptions mentioned in astrological and magical texts were often shared among common people.

This doesn't mean that everyone back then believed that same-sex desire was innate or biological. I'm not sure if Paul or other New Testament authors believed this. The Bible doesn't talk about an innate same-sex desire springing from one's nature. And again, ancient writers certainly didn't understand same-sex orientation in the same way we do today.[16]

At the same time, it doesn't seem accurate to say that "the notion of sexual orientation was absent" in Paul's day and then use this to reinterpret Paul.[17] The evidence shows that the notion of inborn, biologically driven same-sex desires existed in Paul's day.

My second concern with this argument is that it imposes modern (and Western) ethical reasoning onto ancient, Eastern biblical writers. Put simply, biblical writers didn't determine whether a behavior is right or wrong based on the desire that leads to that behavior. The Bible largely focuses on behaviors that are right or wrong, and it considers certain desires—like

---

15. See Kyle Harper, *From Shame to Sin: The Christian Transformation of Sexual Morality in Late Antiquity* (Cambridge, MA: Harvard University Press, 2013), 59–60, on the popularity of astrological texts in the first and second centuries AD.

16. For instance, many of my references above are not talking about a lifelong, fixed, and exclusive same-sex orientation. Some of the references may explain why some men were bisexual—sexually attracted to women *as well as* men.

17. Brownson, *Bible, Sexuality, Gender,* 166, 170.

lust or anger or greed—to also be wrong. But I'm unaware of any passage where a behavior is considered holy simply because some people have a really strong and unchangeable desire to engage in it.

I don't at all want to dismiss how powerful something like a same-sex orientation can be. All I'm saying is that we need to pay close attention to how the New Testament develops its ethical framework. Assuming that Paul wouldn't have said the things he did if he had access to the APA feels a little ambitious to me. It also seems to go against the grain of how the ancient biblical writers thought about sexual ethics.

ROMANS 1:26 ISN'T REFERRING TO FEMALE SAME-SEX SEXUAL RELATIONSHIPS

SUMMARY

This argument is very technical and lives primarily in the ivory towers of academia. I almost didn't want to address it for this reason, but it's actually an important argument with practical ramifications, so it's worth wrestling with. Don't feel bad, though, if it's too technical to follow. You're not alone.

The argument goes like this: Romans 1:26 is often assumed to refer to female same-sex sexual relationships, but it's actually referring to women engaging in nonprocreative forms of sex, like oral and anal sex, with men. Four arguments are given for this interpretation: (1) This is how most early church fathers interpreted the verse. (2) The phrase "against nature"[1] (*para physin*) was commonly used of oral and anal sex between a man and a

---

1. The phrases "against nature" and "likewise" referenced throughout this chapter are taken from the NKJV.

woman. (3) The word "likewise" in 1:27 (where male same-sex relationships are in view) isn't intended to project the same-sex relationships of 1:27 back onto 1:26. And (4) the Greek word *chrēsis* ("use") in 1:26 (i.e., "Even their women exchanged the natural *use* [*chrēsis*] for what is against nature" NJKV) refers to sex acts between men and women, not between two women.[2]

POINTS OF AGREEMENT

I came across this interpretation years ago when I did my first deep-dive study on Romans 1. At first, I didn't think it was plausible. I just thought scholars with too much time on their hands were making stuff up. But after considering all the arguments, I realized that there might be something here. Granted, only a few modern scholars take this view (we'll call it the nonprocreative view). But it's true that several of the earliest interpretations of Romans 1:26 apply it to nonprocreative sex between men and women.

I've also published arguments against the nonprocreative interpretation that weren't as precise as they should have been. Buried in an endnote in my book *People to Be Loved*, I gave four reasons the nonprocreative argument is wrong. I said, for instance, that "the phrase *para physin* ['against nature'] is never used in reference to nonprocreative forms of heterosexual sex in ancient literature, but used on several occasions to describe lesbian

---

2. Whenever *chrēsis* is used to refer to "a sex act, its subject is the man, and the context involves penetration" (David J. Murphy, "More Evidence Pertaining to 'Their Females' in Romans 1:26," *Journal of Biblical Literature* 138, no. 1 [2019]: 221–240 [221]).

sex." I actually got that claim from lesbian scholar Bernadette Brooten, who wrote an entire scholarly book on Roman 1:26 and is an expert on the passage. I did comb through lots of relevant ancient texts and didn't find any use of *para physin* that described nonprocreative male/female sex. But after revisiting the evidence, I have found at least one ancient reference that *does* use *para physin* to describe nonprocreative sex between a man and a woman.[3]

Anyone who's using Romans 1:26 to support their view— whether traditional or affirming—should slow down, do a lot of research, and pay close attention to Paul's actual words. We shouldn't just rely on what this passage seems to mean at first glance.

RESPONSE

Even though I think there's more credibility to the nonprocreative interpretation than I used to believe, I think the same-sex view makes more sense for the following reasons.[4]

---

3. For instance, Diodorus Siculus, a first-century BC historian, refers to a woman who was "incapable of intercourse as a woman," which presumably refers to vaginal intercourse, and "was obliged to submit to unnatural embraces [*ten de para physin homilian*]" (*Library* 32.11); see Diane Swancutt, "Sexing the Pauline Body of Christ: Scriptural Sex in the Context of the American Christian Culture War," in *Toward a Theology of Eros: Transfiguring Passion at the Limits of Discipline,* ed. Virginia Burrus and Catherine Keller (New York: Fordham University Press, 2009), 63–98 (78).

4. Bernadette Brooten spent an entire book arguing for the female same-sex view that I'm taking here (*Love Between Women: Early Christian Responses to Female Homoeroticism* [Chicago: University of Chicago Press, 1996]). She's also addressed the question of how this verse was interpreted by the early church—a question I'm not going to address here for the sake of space. In short, the early church's interpretation was mixed (see Bernadette Brooten, "Patristic Interpretations of Romans 1:26," in *Studia Patristica XVIII: Papers of the 1983 Oxford Patristics Conference* [1985], ed. Elizabeth Livingstone, 287–91).

First, the phrase *para physin* ("against nature") almost always refers specifically to same-sex sexuality in Greco-Roman and Jewish literature. Even writers who condemn nonprocreative heterosexual sex don't typically use the phrase *para physin* to do so. Instead, *para physin* is almost always used as a stock phrase for same-sex sexual acts. It's not impossible that Paul used *para physin* to refer to nonprocreative forms of sex; again, I have found at least one example in ancient literature along these lines. But the dominant usage of *para physin* certainly describes same-sex sexual behavior.

Second, the word "likewise" in 1:27 suggests that 1:26 is talking about female same-sex sexual relationships. Everyone agrees that 1:27 is talking about male same-sex sexual relationships. So, since 1:27 is connected to 1:26 with the word "likewise," this shows that 1:26 is also talking about same-sex sexual relationships and not nonprocreative heterosexual ones.

I do want you to know, however, that New Testament scholar Jamie Banister has argued against this logic. Banister wrote a lengthy article on the Greek word translated "likewise" (*homoiōs*) in Romans 1:27 and tried to show that just because 1:27 is talking about same-sex sexual behavior does not mean that 1:26 is.[5] Banister looked at other uses of *homoiōs* in ancient literature and found that nowhere is *homoiōs* used to explain an ambiguous statement by following it up with a clarifying one. In

---

5. See Jamie A. Banister, "*Homoiōs* and the Use of Parallelism in Romans 1:26–27," *Journal of Biblical Literature* 128, no. 3 (2009): 569–90.

other words, Banister argues that Paul isn't mentioning same-sex acts in 1:27 *in order to explain* the less clear statement in 1:26.

But Banister's point assumes that *Paul* thought Romans 1:26 wasn't very clear and needed 1:27 to explain it. Modern interpreters may debate the meaning of Romans 1:26—as they do every verse in Scripture. But this doesn't mean Paul himself thought his words in 1:26 were particularly ambiguous. Paul could just be using the term "likewise" in 1:27 to connect the logic of 1:26 to 1:27, not to make 1:27 explain 1:26. It just seems most natural to read the two passages in tandem.

Third, Paul's use of "natural relations" connects 1:26 to 1:27 and suggests that both are talking about same-sex sexual relations. Look at the language again:

> Their women exchanged **natural relations** (*tēn physikēn chrēsin*) for those that are contrary to nature; and the men likewise gave up **natural relations** (*tēn physikēn chrēsin*) with women and were consumed with passion for one another, men committing shameless acts with men and receiving in themselves the due penalty for their error.[6]

No one disputes that 1:27 is talking about same-sex sex and that "natural relations" refers to opposite-sex sex—the thing they

---

6. I'm using the ESV translation, since it's closer to the original than the NIV here.

abandoned. I think it's reasonable, then, to say that "natural relations" in both verses refers to the same thing—opposite-sex relationships—and that these were given up for the same thing—same-sex relationships. No one doubts that this is what Paul means in 1:27; "natural relations" (*tēn physikēn chrēsin*) refers to opposite-sex relationships, which men gave up *for* same-sex relationships. Saying that Paul isn't thinking of same-sex relationships in 1:26 while maintaining that he is thinking of them in 1:27 creates more problems than it solves in Paul's argument.

Last, it's unlikely that Paul is condemning females for choosing anal sex over vaginal sex while the men involved in the act don't get a word from Paul. Look at the wording in 1:26; it's the women, not the men, who are condemned. To put it plainly, the logic of the nonprocreative argument says that the men were very much eager to engage in vaginal sex but it was the *women* who instead desired anal sex and forced men into these kinds of sex acts. I mean, really? We have lots of examples in Greco-Roman literature—too many, actually—of men having anal sex with women and receiving oral sex from women. Simply the existence of these sex acts is not the point. What the nonprocreative view argues is that women were the guilty agents, the culprits, the main ones responsible for preferring anal and male-pleasing oral sex over vaginal sex. I want to say, "Only a man would believe this interpretation," but I'll refrain.

Now, classics scholar David Murphy does believe this interpretation and even wrote a technical article defending the nonprocreative interpretation. One of the main arguments he gives is that whenever *chrēsis* (translated as "relations" in 1:26 and 1:27, sometimes translated as "use") occurs in ancient literature to refer to a sex act, "its subject is the man, and the context involves penetration."[7] His article is dense and hard to understand, so I want to be careful not to misrepresent him. In fact, the article is available for free online, so I encourage you to fact-check my interpretation to make sure I'm conveying his points correctly. Here's a summary of his argument; I'll quote it in full and then explain its significance:

> We are justified, then, to conclude that Paul and his readers would not expect *chrēsis* as used in Rom 1:26–27 to denote a female's "use of " anyone in a sex act. Paul looks at intercourse from the point of view, first, of the penetrated female, and then from that of the penetrating male. Only the male has "use of " the other partner. In "natural" *chrēsis*, the females are penetrated by males, and they do not have "use" of anyone. In "unnatural" *chrēsis*, the females again are penetrated by males, and again they do not have "use" of anyone. They have only switched the orifice they present for penetration. They are the subjects of the exchange but not subjects of *chrēsis*.[8]

7. Murphy, "More Evidence," 221.
8. Murphy, "More Evidence," 228.

If you're feeling an interpretive buzz right now, you're probably not alone. What Murphy is saying is that, in Paul's world, the word *chrēsis* always describes male/female penetrative sex, not female/female nonpenetrative sex.[9] So the end of 1:26 can't be describing female/female sex, since there is no penetrator. While I'm not sure that Paul is really focusing on such nitty-gritty details as certain women who "switched the orifice they present for penetration," Murphy's argument might be the best case against the same-sex interpretation. However, I do see at least three hurdles to Murphy's interpretation.

First, a word's meaning is determined, in part, by the context in which it's used, not simply by how the word is used elsewhere. Certainly, looking at how *chrēsis* is used elsewhere is important, but it's not the sole factor for determining what Paul means by the word here. Second, and related, I think the other points I offered above for the same-sex interpretation are contextual reasons that Paul is using *chrēsis* to describe same-sex sex, even if this isn't the typical way in which other writers used the word. In other words, Murphy's view needs to make better sense of 1:26–27 as a whole and not just the meaning of *chrēsis*. Interpreting the "unnatural relations" in 1:26 as referring to male/female nonprocreative sex seems to create more problems than it solves. Third, it might be true that *chrēsis* is never used to describe nonpenetrative same-sex female relations—I haven't verified all of Murphy's references,

---

9. Paul's Greek says that the women exchanged *tēn physikēn chrēsin* ("the natural use") for *tēn para physin* ("that which is against nature"). The noun *chrēsin* is still the understood noun governing the repeated *tēn* of the second phrase, which is where Murphy is getting his argument from.

nor have I done a similar search for all the uses of *chrēsis* in ancient literature. But we do have instances where women are described as having sex like men (from the ancient writer's viewpoint). For instance, the Stoic philosopher Seneca, writing around the same time as Paul, describes women who, "having devised so deviant a type of shamelessness, these women *enter* men,"[10] which not only stretches the imagination but also reflects the idea that some women have sex like men.[11] The word *chrēsis* (or the Latin equivalent) isn't used here, but it's still an example of an ancient author using language typical of male (penetrative) sex and applying it to women. The ancient Roman poet Martial says something similar when he refers to a lesbian named Philaenis who "penetrates young men; and more furious than any husband."[12] Again, a woman is described as having sex like a man.

It's at least possible that Paul is doing something similar here—using language characteristic of male/female penetrative sex (*chrēsis* in particular) and applying it to female same-sex sexual relations. The context of Romans 1 lends support for this interpretation.

Lots of things to digest here. And I'll be the first one to admit that interpreting Romans 1:26 is more complicated than most readers of the English Bible realize. I still think the female

---

10. Seneca, *Moral Epistles* 95.21.

11. On which see Joseph R. Dodson, "The Fall of Men and the Lust of Women in Seneca's *Epistle* 95 and Paul's Letter to the Romans," *Novum Testamentum* 59, no. 4 (2017): 355–65.

12. Martial, *Epigrams* 7.67; cf. 7.70.

same-sex interpretation of this verse makes the most sense of Paul's logic and wording in this passage. And if this is correct, then this would add further support for Paul prohibiting adult, consensual, same-status, same-sex sexual relationships, since these were typical among some women in the ancient world.

THE WORD *HOMOSEXUAL* WAS ADDED TO THE BIBLE IN 1946

SUMMARY

This argument says that the term *homosexual* is an inaccurate translation of the Greek words *arsenokoitēs* and *malakoi*) used in 1 Corinthians 6:9 and 1 Timothy 1:9–10—two of the five prohibition passages. In fact, nowhere does the Bible in its original languages use a term that should be translated as "homosexual" or "homosexuality." Modern translations that use these terms are inaccurate, and the results of this mistranslation have been devastating. This mistranslation says that the Bible condemns gay people simply for being gay.

This argument has become so popular that there's a recent documentary called *1946: The Mistranslation That Shifted a Culture*, which tells the story about this mistranslation. "The first time the word 'homosexual' appeared in any bible," says the documentary's website, "was in the *Revised Standard Version*

(RSV) published in February 11, 1946."[1] The RSV's translation of 1 Corinthians 6:9–10 thus read:

> "Or do you not know that the unrighteous will not inherit the kingdom of God? Do not be deceived; neither the immoral, nor idolaters, nor adulterers, nor **homosexuals** ... will inherit the kingdom of God.

"Today, the misuse of the word 'homosexual' appears in most translations of the Bible.... Sadly, this has become the foundation for much of the anti-gay culture that exists today, especially in religious spaces."[2]

POINTS OF AGREEMENT

This argument is easy to applaud, since it's 100 percent accurate. The word *homosexuals* is a problematic translation of 1 Corinthians 6 (and any other passage where it may be used) in light of how the term *homosexuals* is understood today.[3] The Greek

---

1. "What If the Word 'Homosexual' Was Never Meant to Be in the Bible?," *1946*, www.1946themovie.com.

2. "What If the Word 'Homosexual,'" *1946*.

3. From a strictly linguistic perspective, it seems clear why some translations have "homosexuals" for *arsenokoitēs*. The Greek noun simply means "one engaging in homosexual acts" (specifically, a male having sex with a male), so the substantivization of a participle creates this noun—"homosexual." Similarly, the noun form of "one who runs" would be "runner." The problem, as we'll see, is that the term "homosexual" today typically means "one who is attracted to the same sex," not one who is necessarily engaging in same-sex sexual behavior.

word *arsenokoitēs* translated as "homosexuals" by the 1946 version of the RSV does not mean "homosexuals." The modern English word *homosexual* refers to someone who is sexually attracted to someone of the same sex. But this isn't what *arsenokoitēs* means. *Arsenokoitēs* is best translated as "men who have sex with males"; that is, it refers to sexual *behavior,* not sexual *attraction.* But *homosexual* refers to attraction.

Traditional Christians, please take note: The results of this mistranslation are truly horrific. Think about it. Someone can be "homosexual" and still follow the historically Christian view of marriage. (I don't love the term *homosexual* and use the term *gay* instead, but since *homosexual* is the term under question here, I'll continue to use it.) I know several gay people who believe that gay sex is sin, so they abstain from having gay sex. But they're still "homosexual"—attracted to the same sex. My friend Greg is a passionate follower of Jesus, a brilliant thinker and beautiful writer. My kids know him as "Uncle Greg" and absolutely adore him, not only because he's one of the most delightful and kindest humans you'll ever meet but, most of all, because he radiates the beauty and holiness of Christ whenever he enters a room. Greg is gay. And Greg has devoted his life to celibacy out of allegiance to Jesus. And yet, the 1946 version of the RSV says that Greg—a "homosexual"—"will not inherit the kingdom of God." Goodness. If Greg doesn't make it in, then we're all pretty much nixed.

But that's not what the Greek text of 1 Corinthians 6 and 1 Timothy 1 says. It says that same-sex sexual *behavior* is sin (along with all sex outside of marriage), not same-sex attraction.

RESPONSE

I could go on and on praising this argument, because it's such an important one. There is one major flaw in it, though—not so much in the argument itself but in how it is sometimes used. It's absolutely right to say that the Bible never uses the word *homosexual*. But it would be wrong to say that the Bible *therefore* doesn't say that marriage is between male and female or that same-sex sexual relationships are *therefore* morally permissible. At the end of the day, this argument doesn't really do anything to advance the affirming view of same-sex *marriage*. It just rightly corrects a botched interpretation of two important passages, freeing us from wrongly condemning gay people simply for experiencing same-sex attraction.

So what is the best way to translate *arsenokoitēs* in 1 Corinthians 6:9 and 1 Timothy 1:9–10, if it doesn't mean "homosexual"? If you scan English translations, you'll see that many of them differ. There's actually been quite a debate over how best to translate the word. I've addressed this more thoroughly elsewhere, so let me summarize the gist of the issue.[4]

Paul is the first writer to ever use the term *arsenokoitēs*; he seems to have coined it. But the term is a compound word made up of two other Greek words: *arsen* ("male") and *koitē* ("bed"). By itself, the compound word basically means "one who goes to bed with a male" or "one who has sex with a male." But we have to be careful not to assume too much about compound

---

4. See my *People to Be Loved: Why Homosexuality Is Not Just an Issue* (Grand Rapids, MI: Zondervan, 2015), 103–20.

words. *Pineapple* has nothing to do with apples or pine. Other compound words are more straightforward (*fireplace* means just that). Significantly, the two words *arsen* and *koitē* both occur in the Greek translation of Leviticus 18:22 and 20:13, where male same-sex sexual relationships are forbidden:

> Leviticus 18:22
>
> *kai meta **arsenos** ou koimēthēsē **koitēn** gynaikeian*
> "and you shall not lie with a **male** with the **lying** of a woman"

> Leviticus 20:13
>
> *kai hos an koimēthē meta **arsenos** **koitēn** gynaikos ...*
> "and whoever lies with **a male** as one **lies with** a woman ..."

Paul's compound word *arsenokoitēs* seems to be drawn from these two passages, especially Leviticus 20:13, where the two words occur side by side. The best translation of *arsenokoitēs*, therefore, is "a man who has sex with a male." This is exactly what the two words *arsen* and *koitē* mean in the original context in which they occur (Lev. 18 and 20).

So, while *homosexual* (or gay person) is *not* a good translation of *arsenokoitēs*, the word still does refer to same-sex sexual relationships. While the 1946 RSV wrongly condemned gay people simply for being gay, it's not responsible for promoting some alleged false belief about sex difference being part of what marriage is. That much we get from many other passages and theological themes in Scripture.

For what it's worth, the RSV was updated in 1971, and it no longer uses the word *homosexuals* to translate 1 Corinthians 6:9. In fact, few translations do. The KJV doesn't say "homosexuals" but "abusers of themselves with mankind." I don't even know what that means. The old NIV translation from 1984 used the phrase "homosexual offenders," which could mean that Christians should stop offending homosexuals. (Thanks to Justin Lee for that one!) The NKJV and the NASB are the only current popular English translations I know of that still say "homosexuals" in 1 Corinthians 6:9. (For what it's worth, I've googled my heart out to find an online version of the 1946 edition of the RSV, but I can't find one.) I think the 2020 CSB contains the best translation of these passages: "males who have sex with males."[5]

I'm not sure how much homophobia has been spawned from conservative Christians simply reading the RSV or other translations. I'm sure it's done some damage. And again, I think it really bungled the meaning of 1 Corinthians 6 and 1 Timothy 1. I do think, though, that English-speaking Christians have other, more biblical reasons for believing that marriage involves sex difference and that all sexual relationships outside of this relationship are sin.

---

5. The older version of the CSB translated 1 Timothy 1:10 with "homosexuals," but the 2020 CSB now has "males who have sex with males."

THE BIBLICAL WRITERS WERE PRODUCTS OF THEIR HOMOPHOBIC AND PATRIARCHAL CULTURE

SUMMARY

I've seen this argument take two different forms. The first one is more popular, the second more academic.

The popular approach says that the biblical world was profoundly patriarchal, misogynistic, and homophobic, and so were the biblical writers. They assumed that everyone was heterosexual and that to engage in same-sex sexual activity was downright disgusting. They didn't just believe that same-sex sexual relations were wrong. They believed that people who engaged in such behavior were particularly wicked. When we moderns read the Bible, we can still find many ethical teachings to follow, like "love your neighbor" and "give to the poor." But when it comes to moral teachings that are tethered to patriarchal and homophobic assumptions—like the same-sex prohibitions—we should discard them.

The academic version of this argument is a bit more nuanced. It recognizes two different views toward women and patriarchy in Scripture. One strand of thought highlights equality (like Gen. 1:27 or Gal. 3:28), while another highlights hierarchy (like 1 Cor. 11:9 or Eph. 5:22). The biblical authors were slowly moving away from the hierarchical view and toward more equality after Christ's resurrection. While the dominant and more authoritative strand in the New Testament is equality, we still have statements that reflect patriarchy and misogyny in the New Testament—including the same-sex prohibitions. According to James Brownson, "At least some of the biblical prohibitions and negative portrayal of same-sex eroticism were clearly linked to assumptions regarding patriarchy: what made such an act wrong, at least in large part in these texts, was that it was regarded as inherently degrading to treat a (higher-status) man as if he were a (lower-status) woman."[1]

When modern Christians read and follow the Bible, this argument proposes, we should strip it of its misogynistic, patriarchal, and homophobic assumptions. Since these assumptions form the moral logic of the same-sex prohibitions, we should shed

---

1. James Brownson, *Bible, Gender, Sexuality: Reframing the Church's Debate on Same-Sex Relationships* (Grand Rapids, MI: Eerdmans, 2013), 83. Regarding Romans 1, Brownson writes, "Male-male sex in particular was 'unnatural' because it degraded the passive partner into acting like a woman" (*Bible, Gender, Sexuality*, 245; cf. 237). Likewise, affirming scholar Daniel Helminiak says that "unnatural" does not mean that an act is wrong "according to the universal laws of nature"; rather, it simply means to act "unexpectedly" or "in an unusual way" (*What the Bible Really Says about Homosexuality* [San Francisco: Alamo Square, 1994], 79).

these as well. Bill Loader writes, "It is not disrespectful of writers of Scripture and, in particular, of Paul, to suggest that their understanding of human reality needs to be supplemented."[2]

POINTS OF AGREEMENT

This argument makes many good observations about the social complexity of the biblical world. Our response to this argument shouldn't be reactionary, defending everything the Old Testament says about women: "No, the patriarch *should* give his teenage daughter in marriage to an older man, and brothers *should* marry their widowed sister-in-law to raise up seed for the deceased." Not everything in the Bible should be applied to contemporary Christians in the same way it was given in its ancient context. As John Walton likes to say, the Bible wasn't written *to* us, but it was written *for* us.[3] The Bible was certainly written in a different cultural context, and sometimes really depraved cultural norms of the day are entangled with some biblical commands, particularly in the Old Testament.

As far as the historical context goes, this argument has a lot of merit. The cultural belief that the passive partner in male same-sex relations is feminized is well documented in the literature. The elder Curio, for instance, quips that Julius Caesar was "every

---

2. William Loader, "The Bible and Homosexuality," in *Two Views on Homosexuality, the Bible, and the Church*, ed. Preston Sprinkle (Grand Rapids, MI: Zondervan, 2016), 47.

3. Walton has said this in so many places that there's even a book with this phrase as the title in his honor: Adam E. Miglio et al., eds., *For Us, but Not to Us: Essays on Creation, Covenant, and Context in Honor of John H. Walton* (Eugene, OR: Pickwick, 2020).

woman's man and *every man's woman*," referring to Caesar's role as the passive partner with the Bithynian king Nicomedes.[4] Cicero mocks Mark Antony for being a "common whore" and later a "wife" to the younger Curio on the same grounds.[5] The moral logic of these statements suggests that men should act like the superior men they are, while women should remain in their inferior role as the receptive partner. When a man acts like a passive woman in intercourse, he loses his man card.

I'll focus on this more academic and nuanced version of the argument, since it's really the better of the two. Plus, both versions end up saying essentially the same thing: the moral logic driving the same-sex prohibitions is outdated.

RESPONSE

There are two lines of reasoning that fuel this argument: the Bible's historical context and the biblical text itself. Regarding the historical context, James Brownson believes that "the dominant, penetrating male was *always* older versus younger, free versus slave, of higher status versus lower status."[6] If this was *always* true, then we might assume that Paul too reflected this Greco-Roman patriarchal disdain for same-sex sexual relations.

But as we've already seen (Conversations 4 and 5), there was some diversity in how same-sex relations were viewed, especially in

---

4. Curio the elder, quoted in Suetonius, *Jul.* 52.3 (emphasis mine).
5. Cicero, *Phil.* 2.44–45.
6. Brownson, *Bible, Sexuality, Gender*, 82 (emphasis mine).

the first century. Yes, most male same-sex sexual relationships followed the active/passive, or dominant/dominated, paradigm. But in Paul's day, there were a growing number of exceptions to this. Roman historian Laura Dunn has shown that "in the late Republic and the early Empire this cultural model [strict active and passive roles] was apparently under attack."[7] What's interesting is that there were many erotic wall paintings discovered at Pompeii—the city near Rome that was destroyed by a volcanic eruption in the first century—and the sex scenes are very diverse. They "depict adult males playing passive roles with women and with men; and many authors speak of women who were no longer conforming to passive, subordinate roles in sex acts or in marriage."[8] Even Nero, the leader of the empire in Paul's day, played the passive role in one of his public marriage ceremonies. Sexual norms and taboos were breaking apart in the first century, so we can't assume all same-sex sexual relationships strictly followed earlier cultural norms and then assume that's all Paul would have had in mind.

And as we've seen (Conversations 4, 5, and 7), female same-sex relationships didn't follow the active/passive paradigm that many male relations did. So it's unlikely that Paul's alleged patriarchal sensibilities were offended by lesbian sex. The patriarchal argument can only work if Romans 1:26 is *not* talking about female same-sex sexual relations. This is probably why James Brownson assumes (without much evidence) that Romans 1:26 is

---

7. Laura A. Dunn, "The Evolution of Imperial Roman Attitudes toward Same-Sex Acts" (PhD diss., Miami University, 1998), 311–12.

8. Dunn, "Evolution of Imperial Roman Attitudes," 311–12.

referring to anal or oral sex between heterosexual couples, not to female same-sex sexual relations.

But let's follow Brownson's logic that "the dominant, penetrating male was *always* older versus younger, free versus slave, of higher status versus lower status." It isn't actually true that this was *always* the case, but let's just assume it is for a second. We still have to show that Paul is agreeing with his misogynistic culture rather than departing from it. It's one thing to say, "This is common in Paul's culture"; it's another to say, "This is common in Paul."[9]

Romans 1:26–27 doesn't give much evidence that Paul is flashing his misogynistic card in condemning same-sex sexual relationships. As many scholars recognize, he alludes to Genesis 1–3 throughout Romans 1:18–32, suggesting that same-sex relationships (along with many other sins listed in the chapter) are a violation of the created order.[10] For instance, Paul describes

---

9. Paul's use of *malakoi* in 1 Corinthians 6:9 is sometimes cited as an example of Paul actually agreeing with his culture. The word *malakoi* was sometimes used as a slur for effeminate men who acted like "inferior women" (from an ancient perspective). The patriarchal argument suggests that the *reason* Paul thought *malakoi* were in sin is that the passive male was subjecting himself to be treated as a "mere woman." We could assume that such intentions are lying behind Paul's words, but it's certainly not that clear. Paul simply gives us two words without further context, so we should be cautious in assuming we know Paul's intentions. Paul could very well be using a term familiar to his audience without necessarily believing that the passive partner is wrong *because* he's acting like an "inferior woman." It's just difficult to squeeze Paul's alleged intentions out of two Greek words without much context.

10. Paul's entire argument in Romans 1 has deep roots in the creation account. God, who is called "the Creator" (v. 25), has been revealing himself "since the creation of the world" (v. 20). Moreover, the use of *thēleiai* and *arsenes* in Romans 1:26–27 almost certainly alludes to LXX Genesis 1:27, and Romans 1:23 clearly echoes Genesis 1:26. Less clear, though probable, connections between Romans 1 and Genesis 1–3 are references to "a lie" (Rom. 1:25; cf. Gen. 3:1), shame (Rom. 1:27; cf. Gen. 3:8), knowledge (Rom. 1:19, 21, 28, 32; cf. Gen. 2:17; 3:5), and the sentence of death (Rom. 1:32; cf. Gen. 2:17; 3:4–5, 22).

men and women with the terms *thēleiai* ("females") and *arsenes*
("males") in Romans 1:26–27, which almost certainly refer back
to Genesis 1:27, the first and most significant biblical passage
where these two words occur together. Genesis 1:27, of course, is
a profound statement about the *full equality of men and women*—
both are created in the image of God. It seems unlikely that Paul
would allude to a passage about women's full equality in order to
make an argument rooted in women's inferiority.

It doesn't seem clear to me that Paul is emulating the misogyny of his Greco-Roman culture. Romans 1 and 1 Corinthians 6
read quite differently from, say, Curio, who called Julius Caesar
"every woman's man and *every man's woman*," or Seneca, who
said that the passive male will "never be allowed to become a
man" since he takes "the passive role with another man."[11] The
alleged misogyny of Paul just doesn't seem to leap off the pages
as it does with these other authors. In fact, classicist Kyle Harper
has spent a lot of time in the Greco-Roman literature and how it
views same-sex sexual relationships, where power differentials and
intrinsic misogyny are clear. But when it comes to Paul, "the very
language of 'males' and 'females' stood apart from the prevailing
idiom of 'men' and 'boys,' 'women' and 'slaves.' By reducing the
sex act down to the most basic constituents of male and female,
Paul was able to redescribe the sexual culture surrounding him in
transformative terms."[12] Harper concludes, "What is significant

---

11. Seneca, *Moral Epistles* 122.7.

12. Kyle Harper, *From Shame to Sin: The Christian Transformation of Sexual Morality in Late Antiquity* (Cambridge, MA: Harvard University Press, 2013), 95.

about early Christian moralizing, from Paul onward, is that it drew so little from established modes of criticism."[13] In other words, we can't just map Greco-Roman cultural assumptions onto Paul.

When we look at Paul himself, I really don't think he was as misogynistic as some think he was. He calls several women "co-workers" (Rom. 16:3–4; Phil. 4:3), workers in the Lord (Rom. 16:6, 12), "deacon" (Rom. 16:1–2; 1 Tim. 3:11), and prophets (1 Cor. 11:5; cf. Acts 21:9), and he calls Phoebe, who apparently funded much of the early Christian mission, a "patron" (Rom. 16:2 ESV). He calls Junia an "apostle" (Rom. 16:7) and boldly states that in Christ there is "neither male nor female" (Gal. 3:28 NASB). And I'm unaware of any Greco-Roman writer who says that women have just as much authority over their husbands' bodies as their husbands have over theirs (1 Cor. 7:3–5).

Even passages like Ephesians 5:21–33, where wives are told to submit to their husbands (along with all believers submitting to "one another," v. 21), don't reflect the blatant misogyny of Paul's world. Aristotle once said that "the relation of male to female is by nature a relation of *superior to inferior and ruler to ruled*."[14] Does that sound like Paul? Paul never says that women are *inferior* to men. Arius Didymus says that "the deliberative [reasoning] faculty in a woman is inferior, in children it does not yet exist, and in the case of slaves it is completely absent."[15] Jewish

---

13. Harper, *From Shame to Sin*, 99.
14. Aristotle, *Politics* 1.5.7.
15. Arius Didymus, *Concerning Household Management* 148.14–18.

author Josephus writes, "The woman, it [the Law] says, is in all things inferior to the man. Let her accordingly be obedient" to her husband.[16] These authors may have been able to contribute to the script of *The Handmaid's Tale*, but I think Paul would have jumped ship on this gig. Paul does say, "Wives, submit to your husbands" as part of a Christian ethic where all believers are to submit to one another (Eph. 5:22 CSB), but he never says that *women are inferior to men*. Christian submission, of course, is rooted in the life and rhythm of Jesus, who submitted to the Father and was therefore highly exalted to rule over all things (Phil. 2:5–11). Not exactly what you find with Greco-Roman writers who talk about submission.

Even if we follow a very conservative interpretation of Paul's most patriarchal-sounding statements (1 Cor. 11:3; Eph. 5:22–23; Col. 3:18)—and I'm not saying we should—he still doesn't reflect the kind of reasoning of his ancient compatriots, who believed that women were intrinsically inferior to men. I think it's tough to assume, without clear textual evidence, that misogyny is what's fueling his negative comments about same-sex sexual relationships. Compared to other writers who also condemn same-sex behavior, Paul might as well have been a second-wave feminist.

I think this argument raises some good points to consider; I want to keep mulling over it to see if I'm missing something, and you should too. Even though it's a heavy argument and quite

---

16. Josephus, *Against Apion* 2.24.

academic, it's worth slowing down and analyzing so that we can have a better understanding of what the Bible is actually saying. Even though I'm not terribly convinced of the argument, it has helped me fine-tune my understanding of Paul's social context and explore the moral logic of Paul's ethical reasoning.

JESUS NEVER MENTIONED HOMOSEXUALITY

SUMMARY

This argument points out that Jesus never mentioned homosexuality or same-sex sexual relationships. His silence on the matter is taken in one of two ways. Some argue that Jesus' love for marginalized people suggests that he would have affirmed the sanctity of a loving, consensual same-sex sexual relationship. Others say that even if we can't say Jesus would have affirmed same-sex relationships, he seems to have been indifferent to the issue since he never mentioned it. "Given that Jesus said nothing on the topic of same-gender sexual relationships," writes New Testament scholar William Countryman, "the most one can say is that we do not know whether he would have regarded them as contrary to the created order."[1]

---

1. L. William Countryman, *Dirt, Greed, and Sex: Sexual Ethics in the New Testament and Their Implications for Today*, rev. ed. (Minneapolis: Fortress, 2007), 246, quoted in Darrin W. Snyder Belousek, *Marriage, Scripture, and the Church: Theological Discernment on the Question of Same-Sex Union* (Grand Rapids, MI: Baker, 2021), 79.

POINTS OF AGREEMENT

I was once asked by a student of mine, "What does the Bible say about homosexuality?" This was before I had even dug into the question. I said something like, "Go read the red letters of Jesus, and you'll get your answer"—assuming that Jesus condemned homosexuality all over the place. "But Jesus never mentions homosexuality," quipped the astute and somewhat smart-alecky student. I thought he was joking. But then I googled it and found out that he was right. Jesus never once mentioned homosexuality.

Any time an argument drives you back to the text to discover that your assumptions about the Bible were wrong, this should be celebrated. But what are we to make of this argument?

RESPONSE

Historically speaking, there's no reason why Jesus needed to address same-sex sexual relationships. Every Jew in Jesus' day condemned all forms of same-sex sexual behavior. If you examine all the statements made by ancient Jewish writers five hundred years on either side of Jesus (500 BC–AD 500), you won't find any statement by any Jewish writer that comes close to affirming same-sex sexual behavior. Every time it's mentioned, it's condemned.[2]

---

2. See Josephus (*Ant.* 1.200–201; *Against Apion* 2.273–75), Philo (*Laws* 3.37–42; *Contemplative Life* 59–60), *Pseudo-Phocylides* (3, 190–92, 213–14), *Sibylline Oracles* (3.184–87, 5.166), *Letter of Aristeas* (152), 2 Enoch (34:1–2), and later rabbinic literature (*m. San.* 7:4; *t. Abodah Zarah* 2:1; 3:2).

Such widespread agreement in Judaism is remarkable given the diversity of Jewish views on all kinds of topics. For instance, some Jews loved the temple, while others thought it was corrupt.[3] Some regarded the entire Old Testament as authoritative, while others said only the Pentateuch was inspired.[4] Some believed in angels, while others didn't.[5] Some believed in an afterlife, while others denied life after death.[6] And on and on it goes.

Certain aspects of sexual ethics were also disputed. Some condemned intermarriage, while others were okay with it. Some believed that sex and procreation would exist in the new age, while others anticipated an abstinent afterlife.[7] And, of course, there was the well-known debate about divorce.

If you asked ten ancient Jews about twenty different ethical topics, you'd probably get forty-two different answers. Diversity ruled the day. But when it came to same-sex sexual relations, there was no dispute: every single Jew thought they were morally wrong.

Jesus was a Jew, and in the Gospels, he almost always addressed issues that were disputed within Judaism or issues that he wished to correct. The fact that we have no written record of Jesus mentioning same-sex sexual relations is most likely because the question never came up. I mean, when's the last time you

---

3. The Sadducees versus the Essenes.

4. The Pharisees versus the Sadducees.

5. Most branches of Judaism versus the Sadducees.

6. There was a wide array of diversity in Jewish beliefs about the afterlife.

7. Philo (*On Rewards and Punishments* 98–105) and *Wisdom* 3:13 were for it, while *Apocalypse of Moses* 28:4; 37:5 and *Sibylline Oracles* 2.238 were against it.

heard a sermon defending the view that the earth is round and not flat or that having sex with someone else's spouse is morally wrong? If you haven't, do you take this to mean that your pastors are indifferent to these questions? Likewise, every Jew agreed that same-sex sexual relationships were morally wrong, and it doesn't appear that Jesus cared to preach to the choir.

Plus, Jesus wasn't silent on the central question in the debate: the question of sex difference in marriage. Jesus affirmed that "the Creator 'made them male and female'" and that these "two will become one flesh" (Matt. 19:4–5; cf. Mark 10:6–8). The question about same-sex sexual relationships is primarily a question about the nature of marriage, and Jesus wasn't silent about that.

Jesus also mentioned and condemned "sexual immorality" (Matt. 15:19; cf. Mark 7:21). The Greek word for "sexual immorality" is *porneia*. It usually referred to prostitution in the ancient world, but in first-century Judaism and Christianity, it came to refer to all forms of sex outside of a male/female marriage.[8] So when Jesus said that sexual immorality (*porneia*) was wrong, this included same-sex sexual behavior.

We should also note that when it came to sexual ethics— remember, there was some diversity within Judaism—Jesus was on the stricter side of the spectrum. There were two main schools of thought in Judaism around the time of Jesus: the school of Hillel and the school of Shammai, named after their respective

---

8. See Kyle Harper, *From Shame to Sin: The Christian Transformation of Sexual Morality in Late Antiquity* (Cambridge, MA: Harvard University Press, 2013), 86–107.

founders. Both believed in the Mosaic law, but they interpreted it differently. The school of Hillel was known for being more lenient, while the school of Shammai was stricter.

When it came to divorce, for instance, Shammai said divorce was never permissible except in cases where the wife had committed adultery. As for Hillel, he said a man could divorce his wife if she simply cooked a bad meal.[9] Jesus seems to have taken the stricter view of Shammai: "Anyone who divorces his wife, except for sexual immorality, and marries another woman commits adultery" (Matt. 19:9). Some say he went even further than Shammai by not allowing divorce at all (Mark 10:2–12; Luke 16:18). Jesus also took a stricter view of adultery when he said, "Anyone who looks at a woman lustfully has already committed adultery with her in his heart" (Matt. 5:28).

Given what we know about Jesus and Jewish sexual ethics, it seems unlikely that he would have been more lenient on the question of same-sex sexual relationships.

But what about Jesus' radical ethic of love? Didn't he tell us to love everybody?

He certainly did. "Love your enemies" (Matt. 5:44) and "love your neighbor as yourself" (Matt. 22:39)—that about covers everybody. But these and other love commands can never be pitted against Jesus' (strict) Jewish sexual ethic. The same Lord who said "love everyone" also said "don't lust," "don't worry," "don't hate," "don't fornicate," "don't be greedy," "don't retaliate,"

---

9. See *b. Gittin* 90a.

and a whole host of other things that confronted, not reaffirmed, our desires.

We'll consider the "love is love" argument in Conversation 19, so we don't need to say much more about it here. But I do want to point out that Jesus-shaped (*agapē*) love must be set alongside, not against, Jesus' sexual ethic. Jesus loved people who fell short of God's holiness—and the further away they were, the more Jesus loved them. But the direction of Jesus' love was always toward holiness, not away from it. Jesus' love knew no bounds and had no leash. Jesus had a high ethical standard yet radically loved people who fell short of it. His love doesn't mean he approves of all our desires and actions. It means he values our humanity enough to help us follow the Creator's design and intent for how we are to live.

When all is said and done, I don't think there's much evidence for Jesus secretly approving of, or being indifferent to, same-sex sexual relationships.

PAUL SAID IT'S BETTER TO MARRY THAN TO BURN (1 COR. 7)

SUMMARY

Paul commended celibacy to those who are called to this, but for those who aren't called to live a life of celibacy, he said that "it is better to marry than to burn with passion" (1 Cor. 7:9). This argument proposes that some gay Christians are called to celibacy, and that's a worthy vocation. But most are not. Therefore, not only is it harmful to force them to live a life that they aren't called to, but it also goes against what Paul says in this verse. Paul says they should marry, and for gay people, this would mean marrying a person of the same sex.

POINTS OF AGREEMENT

Many people reading this argument should resonate with it. Sexual desires are powerful, sometimes all consuming. A desire for romantic intimacy and a lifelong partner is something most humans experience. For some of us, the years between puberty and marriage were strewn with moments or seasons or years of unmet sexual desires and overwhelming frustration. Some of us raised in the church clung to this verse, anticipating the day when God would take Paul's words seriously and satisfy our "burning" with a spouse!

We'll respond to this argument in a second. But if you're a straight Christian who's happily married, and a gay Christian shares this argument with you, please sit down and listen to their heart. Resonate with their concern. Empathize with the theological dilemma they might find themselves in and the potential joy that this verse might bring.

RESPONSE

In terms of the theological strength of this argument, I do see some problems. Let's start by digging into the meaning of the verse itself. Here's what Paul says:

> To the unmarried [*agamos*] and the widows I say: It is good for them to stay unmarried, as I do. But if they cannot control themselves, they should marry, for it is better to marry than to burn with passion. (1 Cor. 7:8–9)

There are several things going on in the verse that aren't always clear when we quickly read the English translation.

First, notice that Paul's giving advice not to all single people but to "the unmarried" (*agamos*) and to "widows." The word for "unmarried" (*agamos*) could refer to anyone who's never been married. But it could also refer to men who were once married, since it's paired with "widows" in this verse. Some interpreters therefore suggest that the unmarried men were likely widowers.[1] Plus, the normal word for people who have never been married is *parthenos*, or "virgin." In fact, Paul uses the word *parthenos* in 7:25–38 when he addresses the never-been-married folk.

Even though Paul might not be thinking of all single people in this verse, let's just assume the principle still applies. I mean, if we sat Paul down and asked him, "What about single people who have never been married and are burning with passion. Should they get married?" He might very well have said, "Yes, they too should get married."

Second, the Greek phrase translated "cannot control themselves" (*ouk egkrateuontai*) is in the present tense and is better translated as *"are not controlling themselves."*[2] That is, Paul is referring to people who *are* having sex. And given the fact that the vast majority of unmarried people (of marital age) and widows/widowers in the first century were betrothed or about to be betrothed, it's likely that the people who *are* having

---

1. See Gordon Fee, *The First Epistle to the Corinthians*, rev. ed. (Grand Rapids, MI: Eerdmans, 2014), 287; Richard B. Hays, *First Corinthians* (Louisville: John Knox, 1997), 118.

2. On this point, see Dani Treweek, "Is Marriage a Remedy against Sin?," April 22, 2022, https://danielletreweek.substack.com/p/is-marriage-a-remedy-against-sin.

sex in 1 Corinthians 7:9 are doing it with a person they are going to marry.[3]

Therefore, Paul is most likely not saying, "If you have a high libido and low self-control, then you should probably go out and find yourself a spouse because you obviously don't have the gift of celibacy." After all, self-control is part of the fruit of the Spirit (Gal. 5:22–23), which all believers have. It's not some special gift given to a select few superpowered Christians "called" to celibacy.

Third, when Paul says, "Each of you has your own gift from God" (1 Cor. 7:7), this most probably does not refer to some kind of "gift of singleness" that a few people have, people who are able to brush off sexual temptation like crumbs on a T-shirt. The gift here simply means the current state that you're in. "In the Bible, the gift of singleness is the state of being single," writes Andrew Bunt, a same-sex attracted Christian committed to celibacy. "If you are currently single, you are experiencing the gift of singleness." Likewise: "If you are currently married, you are experiencing the gift of marriage. Whatever gift we currently have, God will empower us to live it out, but this doesn't make the gift of singleness a superpower."[4]

The last thing to consider about this passage is that Paul talks about a "concession," not an "accommodation." A concession is when someone considers two things as both morally permissible

---

3. In Roman society, it was expected that widows should get remarried within a year of their spouse's death; see Anthony C. Thiselton, *The First Epistle to the Corinthians: A Commentary on the Greek Text* (Grand Rapids, MI: Eerdmans, 2000), 515.

4. Andrew Bunt, "What Is the Gift of Singleness?," *Living Out*, January 12, 2021, www.livingout.org/resources/articles/51/what-is-the-gift-of-singleness.

but one is better than the other. Pepperoni pizza versus vegetarian. As a carnivore, I will choose pepperoni every day of the week. But if the pizza joint said, "We're out of pepperoni. Do you want vegetarian?" I'd grudgingly say yes. I'd make a concession, because any pizza is better than no pizza.

An accommodation is when someone believes that something is truly sinful but, for whatever reason, they allow for the sin to take place. Like eggplant on pizza. This, of course, is wickedness covered in marinara and is on par with murder. But if I were starving to death, I might—*might*—take a slice. I'd make an accommodation. I'd choose the immorality of eggplant on pizza over dying of starvation as the lesser of two evils.

In 1 Corinthians 7, Paul is not arguing for accommodation. He's arguing for concession. Paul makes a concession between two things that are good—a good vocation (marriage) and a better vocation (singleness)—in order to guard against "sexual immorality" (*porneia*, 7:2). Paul is not making an accommodation between something that's morally good and something he believes is sinful. And this is where it gets sticky. Using Paul's logic to argue that gay people should get married to the same sex if they're burning with sexual desire goes against the very moral logic of Paul in this passage. As a first-century Jew, Paul's concept of marriage included sex difference, and as a Jew, he would have considered same-sex sexual relationships to be *porneia*—the very thing he's pastoring people to avoid. Of course, some will say that Paul was homophobic or didn't know about sexual orientation or didn't know about adult consensual same-sex relationships or whatever and that's why he believed that sex difference was part of marriage. But in terms of what Paul actually says in this passage, he's conceding to male/female marriage against the superior vocation of singleness; he isn't saying that anyone burning with sexual passion should satisfy their desire in the relationship they see fit.

So I don't think appealing to 1 Corinthians 7 is strong evidence *for* same-sex marriage. We would have to first prove the morality of same-sex marriage and *then* map that view back onto Paul's logic to draw implications from what Paul says. It doesn't make sense to make Paul say that to avoid sexual immorality, you should engage in sexual immorality. We'd first have to show that Paul didn't believe (or wouldn't have believed) that same-sex sexual relationships were sexually immoral and then go back to 1 Corinthians 7 to reinterpret the passage.

It may be worth pointing out, too, that Paul doesn't always make concessions when sexual passions are aflame. In 1 Corinthians 5, a guy was sleeping with his stepmother, and Paul doesn't say, "They should get married, because they're obviously burning for each other." Both affirming and traditional Christians will agree that sleeping with your stepmother is sexually immoral; it says so right there in Leviticus 18. Paul would never allow, you might say, for a relationship that Leviticus 18 says is immoral just because two people can't control themselves. And this would be correct.

Or what about people who are polyamorous—sexually oriented toward more than one person at a time? Many poly-identified people say that their needs can't be met by just one person. "Paul says that it's better for all of us to marry each other than for us to burn with passion." Should Christians concede to this relationship? And why? "Whose intimacy needs merit pastoral consideration?" asks Darrin Belousek.[5] It's an interesting question to consider.

According to what Paul actually says here, widows and widowers should get married to the person they're having sex with (and probably betrothed to), since they're obviously showing that they're failing to control themselves. But it would go against what Paul is actually saying (and the moral logic that underlies his statement) to suggest that anyone with an unmet sexual or romantic desire is permitted to act on that desire.

---

5. Darrin W. Snyder Belousek, *Marriage, Scripture, and the Church: Theological Discernment on the Question of Same-Sex Union* (Grand Rapids, MI: Baker, 2021), 250.

JESUS' SABBATH HERMENEUTIC INFORMS HOW WE SHOULD INTERPRET SAME-SEX PROHIBITIONS

SUMMARY

This argument is both thoughtful and complex, so I want to spend more space than usual to explain it. I want to represent it correctly, which would be hard to do in two or three sentences. So here's how it goes.

The Bible prohibits same-sex sexual relationships, but like other commands in Scripture, human need is always taken into account. For instance, the Bible says we should not work on the Sabbath, yet Jesus says that when human life is at stake, it's okay to follow the higher law (love your neighbor) at the risk of going against the lower law (rest on the Sabbath).

The biblical authors themselves "demonstrate that even laws that prohibit something cannot be blindly applied" but should be evaluated "on a case-by-case basis," writes Karen Keen, an affirming scholar who champions this argument.[1] And one of the things we should consider in this deliberative process, Keen says, is "attention to human need."[2]

When it came to divorce or keeping the Sabbath, Jesus demonstrated that he factored in human need. There are some cases where the preservation of human life led him to go against what was normally stated in Scripture.

Take the Sabbath, for example. Even though keeping the Sabbath is one of the Ten Commandments and is rooted in the creation account (Ex. 20:8–11; 31:16–17; cf. Gen. 2:1–3), Jesus shows us that "attention to need is necessary to rightly employ" the Sabbath command and other biblical laws.[3] Jesus "gives specific examples, such as helping an animal or a person who is suffering (Matt. 12:9–13), or freeing a man who hasn't walked in thirty-eight years to finally pick up and carry his mat (John 5:5–9)."[4] When it comes to interpreting various biblical laws, "Jesus and the biblical authors applied humanitarian exceptions to the rule."[5]

If we follow Jesus' hermeneutical lead, then, a case can be made that the same-sex prohibitions are lower laws that should be set aside if human need is at stake. Many gay and lesbian

1. Karen Keen, *Scripture, Ethics, and the Possibility of Same-Sex Relationships* (Grand Rapids, MI: Eerdmans, 2018), 201.

2. Keen, *Scripture, Ethics, and the Possibility*, 201.

3. Keen, *Scripture, Ethics, and the Possibility*, 64.

4. Keen, *Scripture, Ethics, and the Possibility*, 64.

5. Keen, *Scripture, Ethics, and the Possibility*, 102.

people aren't called to celibacy, and so they need to get married. According to Jesus, when human life is at stake—in this case, getting married to someone of the same sex is the human need— then we should set aside the lower laws (same-sex prohibitions) for the sake of preserving life.

POINTS OF AGREEMENT

I love how this argument isn't afraid to look at some of the complexities of biblical interpretation. It isn't satisfied with the somewhat lazy "God said it; I believe it; that settles it" approach to Scripture. Instead, it asks, "What did God actually say? And why did he say it? And what about other passages where God said something different?" In other words, it respects Scripture enough to wrestle with it, to ask hard questions and toss easy answers into the sea.

Questions about divorce and the Sabbath are indeed complicated. In the Old Testament, working on the Sabbath warranted the death penalty (Ex. 31:14–15). Not only is this in the Ten Commandments, but it's also rooted in the creation account (Ex. 20:8–11; cf. Gen. 2:1–3). Some say that Jesus never actually violated the biblical Sabbath command; he only went against certain pharisaical interpretations of it. And that might be true. But what do we do with Matthew 12:4, where Jesus says that David and his men "ate the sacred bread" in the tabernacle, *which is not lawful for him or for those with him to eat*" (HCSB)? Jesus goes on to say, "Haven't you read in the Law that on Sabbath days the priests in the temple *violate the Sabbath and are innocent?*" (v. 5 HCSB). It certainly seems like Jesus is advocating for breaking an actual biblical law under certain circumstances.

RESPONSE

I was impressed with this argument when I first came across it. And I commend Karen Keen, its main advocate, for articulating such a fresh and thoughtful viewpoint. In fact, Keen and I exchanged some blog posts a few years ago over her argument, and I appreciate her kind and thorough interaction.[6] I do think there are a few snags, though, with her reasoning.

One is pretty noticeable. Perhaps some of you are already thinking of it. Even if we grant that Jesus is going against a biblical law in what he says about divorce and the Sabbath, this doesn't in itself mean he would do the same with marriage. When it comes to divorce, there are clear tensions about whether divorce is ever permissible, because the Bible reveals clear evidence of such tensions. Deuteronomy 24 is quite lenient on divorce. Ezra 9–10

---

6. Here is my initial review of and response to Keen's book: Preston Sprinkle, "Scripture, Ethics, and the Possibility of Same-Sex Relationships," The Center for Faith, Sexuality & Gender, December 14, 2018, www.centerforfaith.com/blog/scripture-ethics-and -the-possibility-of-same-sex-relationships. Keen responded to my review here: Karen Keen, "Dialogue with Preston Sprinkle on Scripture, Ethics, and the Possibility of Same-Sex Relationships," Karen R. Keen, December 16, 2018, https://karenkeen .com/2018/12/16/dialogue-with-preston-sprinkle-on-scripture-ethics-and-the -possibility-of-same-sex-relationships. I wrote a response to her response here: Preston Sprinkle, "More Thoughts on Scripture, Ethics, and the Meaning of Marriage," The Center for Faith, Sexuality & Gender, December 28, 2018, www.centerforfaith.com /blog/more-thoughts-on-scripture-ethics-and-the-meaning-of-marriage.

even commands divorce. Malachi 2 says "God hates divorce" (according to some translations).

Okay, so these are in the Old Testament and may be products of a bygone covenant. But even the New Testament seems to display some tension about whether divorce is ever allowed (Mark 10 says no; Matthew 19 says it depends; 1 Corinthians 7 says it depends). The relevant question is, Do we see similar tensions in whether marriage is a one-flesh union between two sexually different persons and whether same-sex sexual relations are permissible? We really don't. As we've seen throughout this book, marriage is often described as the one-flesh union between two sexually different persons, and whenever same-sex sexual relations are mentioned, they are always prohibited. We can't say the same thing about divorce. For whatever reason, there is some diversity in Scripture's treatment of divorce. But similar diversity is lacking when Scripture talks about sex difference in marriage and whether same-sex sexual relationships are ever permissible.

Like divorce, the Sabbath command also exhibits some tensions across Scripture. It's clearly binding on Israel, but we have biblical evidence that it *might* not be binding on all New Testament believers (at least, not binding on Gentile believers). Paul seems to say that keeping the Sabbath is a gray area that believers can disagree over (Rom. 14) or something that was part of the Old Testament law but not necessary for new covenant believers (Col. 2). And Jesus himself seems to make exceptions to keeping Sabbath (Matt. 12). For whatever reason, the New Testament opens up some exceptions to keeping the Sabbath.

But we know this because we have actual biblical evidence. And this is where I really struggle with Keen's argument. Just because one command is given exceptions in Scripture doesn't mean other ones are. Laws about adultery or loving your neighbor, for instance, are absolute with no exceptions, while other laws like the ones about divorce and Sabbath keeping are more complex. Even something like lying has some complexity to it: Rahab is commended for lying about hiding the Hebrew spies (Josh. 2:4–7; cf. Heb. 11:31). The point is, I think we should evaluate each command on a case-by-case basis to see if there could be times to set it aside. The burden of proof is on Keen to convince us that Jesus intended his approach to the Sabbath laws to apply to other laws—especially laws about sexual ethics.[7] In short, I don't find any evidence that Jesus (or the New Testament writers) treated the meaning of marriage or same-sex sexual relationships with the same flexibility that they treated laws about the Sabbath or divorce.

My biggest concern with the argument, though, is how it understands marriage (and sex). I think it borders on idolizing it. Jesus does seem to go against the Sabbath command when human life was at stake. But does this parallel set aside what Jesus himself says about marriage? According to the logic of the argument, going without a sexual relationship "can lead to physical

---

7. I hope I'm representing Keen correctly here. In a blog response, she clarifies: "I am not arguing for random, arbitrary discontinuities. I am arguing for a deliberative process for mandates that is based on scriptural precedence and rationale, namely, consideration of human need" (Keen, "Dialogue with Preston Sprinkle"). As I understand her argument, as long as the interpreter perceives *that a law is preventing them from meeting a human need, they could make an exception to it.*

and emotional death" for those who aren't called to celibacy, says Keen.[8] In other words, being married to the person you sexually desire is necessary for human flourishing for some people, perhaps most people. And if some people can't get married to the person they sexually desire, they might even commit suicide.[9] Therefore, according to this argument, we should make an exception to the biblical prohibitions for the sake of preserving the lives of those who cannot live without marriage and sex.

From a pastoral vantage point, Keen raises an important point about how realistic it is for Christians in the twenty-first century to live without having sex with the person they desire. She points out that "evangelicals between ages eighteen to twenty-nine show rates of nonmarital sex at 44–80 percent" and that "people *will* have sex either within marriage or outside of it."[10] I can appreciate Keen's realism about whether Christians will live perfectly pure sexual lives. But as an ethical argument, I don't find it very compelling. We shouldn't determine whether something is morally good based on percentages of self-proclaimed Christians who are observing it.

But I do resonate with the emotional power of sexual desire and the pull toward marriage. We live in a tremendously sexualized society, no doubt. Sex sells, and sex is everywhere, fanning the flame of our desires wherever we go. The thought of a forty-year-old virgin is such a laughable anomaly that we make a romantic

8. Keen, *Scripture, Ethics, and the Possibility*, 71.
9. As she shares on pages 70–71 of her book.
10. Keen, *Scripture, Ethics, and the Possibility*, 74 (emphasis original).

comedy out of it. And it's true in the church too. Anyone raised in the American evangelical church (especially during the purity culture era) knows that Christians assume that marriage is necessary for human flourishing. The church has—unintentionally or sometimes intentionally—adopted an idolatrous view of marriage and sex, one that leaves single people in the dust, wondering if they're incomplete as image bearers of God. The marriage-is-necessary-to-survive narrative is fueled by an unbiblical theology that suggests Jesus himself is doing something wrong.

I agree that it will be extra difficult for people nurtured in this environment not to marry the person they sexually desire. I just have theological problems with this as an argument. As we saw in Foundation 2, the gospel never promises that God will give you a spouse that you desire. To suggest otherwise is to elevate a secular ideology of marriage, romance, and sex above God's blueprint for human flourishing revealed through the New Testament.[11]

I'm also concerned with how this argument understands the meaning of marriage. It assumes that marriage is primarily for companionship and to solve the problem of human loneliness. This is a widespread assumption in the modern Western church. But it reflects a secular view of marriage rather than a biblical one. We talked about this back in Foundation 2, where we discussed several purposes of marriage. Companionship is *part* of how the

---

11. For more on the church's idolatry of marriage and sex, see Cutter Kallaway, *Breaking the Marriage Idol: Reconstructing Cultural and Spiritual Norms* (Downers Grove, IL: IVP Books, 2018), and Danielle Treweek, *The Meaning of Singleness: Retrieving an Eschatological Vision for the Contemporary Church* (Downers Grove, IL: IVP Academic, 2023).

Bible describes marriage, but there are other, more fundamental purposes of marriage. God didn't design marriage to be *the* solution to loneliness.

Humans can live without sex. But we can't live without love and intimacy. And until the church understands the difference, we will continue to fail our gay and same-sex attracted (and all our single) brothers and sisters. We cannot give the (secular) impression that Christians can't live a flourishing life unless we marry the person we're romantically and sexually attracted to and then turn around and tell our gay siblings that they're not allowed to marry the person they're romantically and sexually attracted to. Affirming Christians want to change the last part of that statement; I say we reform the first part.

No one should live without love and intimacy. And love and intimacy are not limited to romantic and sexual relationships.

GOD'S ACCEPTANCE OF GENTILES MIRRORS HOW WE SHOULD ACCEPT LGB PEOPLE

SUMMARY

All throughout the New Testament, Gentiles are welcomed into God's covenant, and they aren't required to keep the dietary laws or to be circumcised. Even though "there are no [Old Testament] texts that support the position of welcoming the Gentiles without circumcision," the apostles in Acts believed that this law should be overruled, since they had witnessed the Spirit's work in the lives of the Gentiles (Acts 10–11).[1] "James has made the remarkable move of allowing the Old Testament to be illuminated and interpreted by the narrative of God's activity in the present."[2] According to this argument, the

---

1. Sylvia C. Keesmaat, "Welcoming in the Gentiles: A Biblical Model for Decision Making," in *Living Together in the Church: Including Our Differences,* Greig Dunn and Chris Ambidge, eds. (Toronto: ABC Publishing, 2004), 39.

2. Keesmaat, "Welcoming in the Gentiles," 39.

welcome of the Gentiles provides modern believers with scriptural precedent for welcoming in gay and lesbian believers who also show the work of the Spirit in their lives—even if it means going against previous biblical commands, like the apostles did with circumcision for the Gentiles.

POINTS OF AGREEMENT

This is an interesting argument that seems to be growing in popularity. It really is shocking that the apostles in Acts (and Paul in his letters) didn't require Gentile converts to be circumcised. It's one thing for the dietary laws to be done away with; those were instituted later on in the law of Moses (Leviticus, etc.). But circumcision was instituted way back when God first made a covenant with Abraham (Gen. 17). There's no evidence in the Old Testament that this law would someday be done away with.

What I love most about this argument is that it's passionate about welcoming people into the church who are shamed and shunned by religious people. This is exactly how the Gentiles were treated in the New Testament. They were shamed and shunned by religious people, and many LGBTQ people certainly know what this feels like. Sylvia Keesmaat makes a challenging point when she writes, "If the lives of gay and lesbian believers display the fruit of the Spirit: love, joy, peace, patience, kindness, goodness, faithfulness, gentleness, self-control [Gal. 5:22–23], then the church needs to acknowledge the work of God in their lives, as such work was recognized in the lives of Gentiles in Acts."[3] Any church that doesn't welcome gay and lesbian believers simply because they aren't straight is not reflecting the radical welcome of Christ. This shouldn't be debated.

The question, however, is not whether the church should welcome gay, lesbian, bisexual, or straight people into the church. The question is, What is the marital and sexual ethic that they're being welcomed into?

RESPONSE

It's that question—the marital and sexual ethics question—that this argument leaves underdeveloped. In fact, the main passage that this argument draws on, Acts 15, explicitly works against the argument. Acts 15 talks about not requiring that Gentiles be circumcised or abide by Jewish dietary laws. But there were four things that Gentile converts were still commanded to do: "abstain from food polluted by idols, *from sexual immorality*, from the meat of strangled animals and from blood" (v. 20; cf. v. 29). The second one, of course, is most relevant for our topic.

The Greek word translated "sexual immorality" is *porneia*, and as we've seen in Conversation 10, *porneia* refers to all forms of sex outside of a male/female marriage, including same-sex sexual relationships. "When you double-click on the term *porneia*," says New Testament scholar Scot McKnight, "it takes you to Leviticus

---

3. Keesmaat, "Welcoming in the Gentiles," 44.

18."[4] This doesn't at all mean that we shouldn't welcome gay and lesbian people into the church. Quite the opposite. It does mean that we can't assume that a Jewish-Christian sexual ethic was being revamped by the apostles, when the very passage at hand reaffirms a traditional sexual ethic.

But let's go back to the four prohibitions mentioned above: "abstain from food polluted by idols, from sexual immorality, from the meat of strangled animals and from blood" (Acts 15:20; cf. v. 29). Several years ago, a renowned New Testament scholar named Richard Bauckham wrote a famous lengthy article on Acts 15.[5] Okay, maybe it was just famous for scholarly geeks. Anyway, people often assume that James and the other apostles in Acts 15 were going against Old Testament law when they came up with their criteria for welcoming Gentiles. But Bauckham pointed out that the four prohibitions aren't arbitrarily mentioned here. They're actually drawn from Leviticus 17–18, a passage that lists *four* criteria for Gentiles living in the land of Israel:

---

4. Scot McKnight, "Did Jesus Talk about Homosexuality?," *Jesus Creed* (blog), April 6, 2015, www.patheos.com/blogs/jesuscreed/2015/04/06/did-jesus-talk-about-homosexuality. The one sex act prohibited in Leviticus 18 that some say is no longer applicable is sex during menstruation (v. 19). Personally, I've yet to see a rock-solid argument for why this prohibition is no longer valid, and any thoughtful Christian shouldn't just assume that since they haven't heard a sermon on sex during menstruation, it's not for today. It is true, however, that we don't see this prohibition repeated in the New Testament. But this doesn't necessarily mean it's *not* still binding. There's also the connection between mixing blood and semen, which might relate more to the purity laws of Leviticus 11–15, which were wrapped up in ancient views about purity and impurity. In short, I'm not suggesting that Leviticus 18:19 is no longer applicable for Christians; I'm only suggesting that this particular prohibition is more complicated than the others in this chapter.

5. See Richard Bauckham, "James and the Gentiles (Acts 15.13–21)," in *History, Literature and Society in the Book of Acts,* Ben Witherington III, ed. (Cambridge: Cambridge University Press, 1996), 154–84.

- Leviticus 17:7–9 prohibits sacrificing to idols.
- Leviticus 17:10–12 prohibits eating blood.
- Leviticus 17:13–14 prohibits eating an animal that was strangled.
- Leviticus 18:6–23 prohibits sexual immorality.

These are the same four things the apostles required Gentile converts to abide by in Acts 15. They're even listed in the same order in Acts 15:29: "You are to abstain from food sacrificed to idols, from blood, from the meat of strangled animals and from sexual immorality." The last prohibition, "sexual immorality," includes the same-sex prohibition in Leviticus 18:22.

The apostles weren't going against Old Testament law to make room for the Gentiles. They were going to the law to see what welcoming Gentiles should look like.

Sylvia Keesmaat, who champions the Gentile argument, doesn't acknowledge the Leviticus 17–18 connection. When it comes to defining *porneia*, she says it "had a wide variety of over-tones: adultery, sex for hire, temple prostitution. All of these ways of behaving betray a sexuality rooted in the idolatrous practices of the empire, a sexuality characterized by promiscuity, instant gratification, and consumption."[6] These would all be included in

---

6. Keesmaat, "Welcoming in the Gentiles," 41. Again, she writes, "The Jerusalem Council called these Gentile believers to a sexuality rooted in commitment and faithfulness, a sexuality that creates and builds up community rather than tearing it apart" ("Welcoming in the Gentiles," 41). This is largely true; commitment and faithfulness are part of a Christian sexual ethic. (I'm not sure failing to build up community, though, would be considered fornication.)

the meaning of *porneia*, but so would same-sex sexual relations, which she doesn't mention.

I love the pastoral heart behind this argument, but it really does suffer from not looking more closely at the main passage used to support it. Again, the main question should never be, Does God accept gay people into the covenant? One hundred percent he does. The main question is, What *is* the marital and sexual ethic that God calls all his covenant people to follow?

THE TRAJECTORY OF WOMEN AND SLAVERY JUSTIFIES SAME-SEX PROHIBITIONS

SUMMARY

A trajectory argument says that the Bible doesn't always give us a complete or fully developed position on all ethical matters. Take slavery, for example. The Bible never comes out and condemns slavery, but we can see some rumblings of the institution being challenged, especially in the New Testament. Same with how the Bible views women. The Old Testament devalues women, but the New Testament is moving toward full equality and liberation. And the same goes for same-sex prohibitions. If we follow the Bible's trajectory, we find it moving toward liberation, welcome, and acceptance. Traditional Christians are treating the Bible the same way pro-slavery Christians did in the nineteenth century—they're cherry-picking a few verses out of context to support their view, while missing the bigger picture of the Bible.

POINTS OF AGREEMENT

The Bible is indeed filled with ethical trajectories—some things are permitted in the Old Testament but prohibited in the New, while others are prohibited in the Old and permitted in the New. And much of what this argument says about slavery and women is, from my vantage point, true. While we don't see an end to slavery in the Bible, the New Testament does seem to be moving in that direction (cf. Philemon). The Bible does the same with women, as we've seen elsewhere in this book. Even if there are some statements in the New Testament that seem to devalue women (it's debated), there does seem to be a trajectory moving toward establishing the full equality of women that we see in Genesis 1.

RESPONSE

The main question, though, is, Do we see a similar trajectory for marriage and same-sex sexual relationships? I don't think we do. Whenever the Bible offers something like a definition or meaning of marriage, sex difference is involved (Gen. 2:23–24). This isn't just an Old Testament thing; it's affirmed by Jesus and the writers of the New Testament (Matt. 19:4–6; Eph. 5:21–33). Whenever the Bible mentions same-sex sexual relationships, they are always prohibited in both the Old and New Testaments (Lev. 18:22; 20:13; Rom. 1:26–27; 1 Cor. 6:9; 1 Tim. 1:9–10). The same trajectory we see with regard to slavery or women doesn't capture how the Bible describes marriage and same-sex sexual expression.

In fact, if a biblical trajectory does exist for sexual ethics, it moves toward greater strictness, not greater openness. Polygamy, for instance, was treated more leniently in the Old Testament, but we see the New Testament moving back toward the creational ideal of one man and one woman (Matt. 19:4–6). Divorce too was allowed in the Old Testament (Deut. 24:1–4), but Jesus explicitly tightened Deuteronomy's looser divorce laws (Matt. 5:31–32; 19:1–10). Adultery is condemned across both Testaments. But in the New, Jesus said that even lust is adultery (Matt. 5:27–30). When the Bible revisits its vision for marriage and sexuality, it moves toward a stricter ethic, not a more permissive one.

Some have compared the traditional view of marriage to how older pro-slavery Christians handled the Bible. Mark Achtemeier calls this "the fragment method." Pro-slavery Christians "pulled out and interpreted apart from the overall witness of the Scriptures ... isolated fragments ... to conclude that their pro-slavery cause was blessed by God."[1] Christians today, he argues, also appeal to "isolated scriptural fragments as they argued to keep women in subordinate roles within both church and society."[2]

I don't disagree with Achtemeier's points about slavery here. I don't even disagree that some Christians do the same to defend their view about same-sex sexual relationships—they pick out five or six prohibition passages and think that settles it. But as I laid out in Foundation 2, a traditional view of marriage is an essential

---

1. Mark Achtemeier, *The Bible's Yes to Same-Sex Marriage: An Evangelical's Change of Heart* (Louisville: Westminster John Knox, 2014), 19.

2. Achtemeier, *Bible's Yes to Same-Sex Marriage*, 19.

part of the biblical story. We see sex difference in marriage woven throughout the fabric of the creation account, and it concludes the story in Revelation 21–22. The union of two different people into "one flesh" correlates with other broader themes about unity in diversity: ethnic reconciliation between Jew and Gentile (Eph. 2:11–22), Christ's love for the church (Eph. 5:21–33), and heaven and earth coming together in the new creation (Rev. 21–22). "The coming together of male plus female," says N. T. Wright, "is itself a signpost pointing to that great complementarity of God's whole creation, of heaven and earth belonging together."[3]

When we widen our lens and consider how sex difference in marriage is wrapped up with the story line of Scripture, the traditional view—at least in its most thoughtful articulations—is closely tied to "the overall witness of the Scriptures." It's a shame that some traditional Christians have homed in on a few prohibition passages and think that's the extent of why marriage should be between a man and a woman.

In sum, it's not enough to identify some ethical trajectories in Scripture and say that a similar trajectory exists for revamping marriage. We would need to find evidence in Scripture for marriage itself moving beyond sex difference.

3. N. T. Wright, "From Genesis to Revelation: An Anglican Perspective," in Helene Alvaré and Steven Lopez, eds., *Not Just Good, but Beautiful: The Complementary Relationship between Man and Woman* (Walden, NY: Plough, 2015), 88.

THE TRADITIONAL VIEW OF MARRIAGE IS HARMFUL TOWARD GAY AND LESBIAN PEOPLE

SUMMARY

This argument is arguably the most popular and most powerful. I don't think I've read a single book or talked to any person who affirms same-sex marriage who doesn't appeal to the harm argument. Since it's so influential, we'll spend some extra time wrestling with it.

Affirming writer Matthew Vines sums it up well: "Non-affirming beliefs about same-sex relationships and transgender people contribute to serious harm in LGBTQ people's lives."[1] According to Vines, studies show that

> lesbian, gay, and bisexual young adults who reported higher levels of family rejection during

---

1. "Experience of Sound Christian Teachings Should Show Good Fruit, Not Bad Fruit," The Reformation Project, accessed December 14, 2022, https://reformationproject.org /case/good-vs-bad-fruit.

adolescence were 8.4 times more likely to report
having attempted suicide, 5.9 times more likely
to report high levels of depression, [and] 3.4
times more likely to use illegal drugs … compared with peers from families that reported no
or low levels of family rejection.[2]

Vines goes on to show that sexual orientation change efforts
have caused incredible harm to gay people. "Efforts to change people's sexual orientation are not just ineffective—they are harmful."[3]

All of this, he argues, is "bad fruit" that results from the
traditional view of marriage and "should lead us to reconsider
the source of that fruit: our interpretation of Scripture."[4] Jesus
taught that a good tree will bear good fruit (Matt. 7:17). Since
the traditional view has caused so much bad fruit toward gay
people, it's probably not part of a good tree.

Some people say they're not using harm to prove that the
traditional view is wrong; rather, seeing all the harm has driven
them back to the text of Scripture to question whether the traditional view is correct. They agree that the Bible is their ultimate
authority, but seeing all the harm has simply led them to question
traditional interpretations of it.

---

2. Vines is quoting here from The Family Acceptance Project's use of "Parents' Rejection
of a Child's Sexual Orientation Fuels Mental Health Problems," 40, no. 3 (March 2009),
www.apa.org/monitor/2009/03/orientation.

3. "The Need for Reform," The Reformation Project, accessed December 14, 2022,
https://reformationproject.org/the-need.

4. "Experience of Sound Christian Teachings," The Reformation Project.

POINTS OF AGREEMENT

This argument is dear to my heart, because many gay friends of mine have been harmed by the church. Drew Harper, a gay man raised in the church, captures the widespread experience of many when he says, "To be homosexual in the American evangelical church … is to be *dead*…. You are an outcast, an orphan, a refugee. A diseased person."[5] Another gay friend of mine says it like this:

> Having what I call "the abomination gospel" drilled into you at such a young age and told you are so "other" that God doesn't want to even try to reach you warps a person's view of both God and themselves. I'm not sure if it is possible to ever truly undo this damaged view of God and self. A self-deprecating inner monologue is part of the DNA of an LGBT+ person who was raised in the church in culture war USA. We are constantly questioning can God really love ME, am I an abomination, etc. No matter how deeply we love God or accept that God's grace extends to us, we still have this undercurrent of self-loathing and shame.[6]

---

5. Brad Harper and Drew Harper, *Space at the Table: Conversations between an Evangelical Theologian and His Gay Son* (Vancouver, WA: Zeal Books, 2016), 43.

6. Personal correspondence.

Story after story, person after person, these testimonies capture how so many gay people have felt after being raised in the church. Without a doubt, the American evangelical church has not been the most hospitable or loving place for the millions of gay people who have sat in its pews.

I 100 percent stand behind the heart of this argument and have spent the last ten years of my life trying to make a difference in how evangelical Christians go about this important and sensitive conversation.

RESPONSE

I would like to raise several points about how this argument is used to disprove the historically Christian view of marriage.

First, what is the *cause* of the harm? Some say that it's the theological teaching that sex difference is part of marriage and that all sexual relationships outside of marriage are sin. This is one possibility. It's true that most parents who kick their gay kids out of the house or force them into conversion therapy also believe in (some form of) a traditional view of marriage. But correlation doesn't prove causation. Some Christians are also blatant racists and might even use the Bible to justify their racist views. But this doesn't therefore mean that the Bible is the problem. Correlation doesn't prove causation.

There are a number of things that could also be causing the harm: ignorance about the complexities of sexuality, fear of "the other," bigotry toward those who have different struggles, social pressure to dislike gay people, twentieth-century perspectives about masculinity that shame anyone who simply experiences same-sex attraction, unscientific and unbiblical assumptions about people "choosing" to be gay. The list could go on and on. There are many possible reasons that some Christians (and non-Christians) act and talk in a way that harms gay and lesbian people. It's also possible, as this argument claims, that a historically Christian sexual ethic is among the culprits. But this would need to be proved, not assumed. It's certainly true that some traditional Christians have harmed some gay people. But this correlation in itself doesn't show that it's their *beliefs* about marriage and sexual ethics that are causing the harm.

Second, I think that broad-brush generalizations are unhelpful and can be harmful in themselves. Here's what I mean.

Sweeping generalizations like "Christians" and "gay people" are very unhelpful—as if every gay person is harmed by every Christian who believes in a traditional sexual ethic. What about the hundreds of thousands of gay people who believe in a historically Christian view of marriage and sexual ethics? They don't say they are harmed by the *theology* they believe in, even if they say they've been hurt by fellow Christians who hold to the same view. They might also say that the Western progressive sexual ethic that affirms same-sex sexual relationships is itself harmful.

It's certainly true that *some* Christians have harmed *some* gay people. It's also true that some non-Christians harm gay people. It's also true that some Christians help gay people. One of my friends has worked with more than five thousand gay people and their families, helping them toward reconciliation, understanding, and love. As a result, he's received countless responses that go something like, "I wanted to kill my self, and now I want to live after talking to you." I once asked my friend how many gay people he thinks would have committed suicide were it not for the pastoral work he did in their life. My friend is super humble, so I had to drag it out of him, but he ended up saying that it's been about five hundred. And my friend passionately believes in a traditional Christian sexual ethic.

Five hundred gay kids saved from suicide by a man who believes that sex difference is part of marriage. Correlation doesn't prove causation.

Some Christians harm gay people. And some Christians help gay people. Some LGB people harm some trans* people, and some trans* people harm some LGB people. Some lesbians accuse biologically male trans people of harming women. Some gay people who convert to Christianity say they have been harmed by a narrative that celebrates same-sex sexual relationships. And on and on it goes. Sweeping statements about broad categories of people are rarely helpful.

Rather than assuming certain things about people who hold certain viewpoints, we should examine the veracity of the viewpoints themselves.

Let's test the harm argument with a different scenario: straight people who have sex outside of marriage. Some traditional Christians who believe that sex outside of marriage is wrong have harmed people who have had sex outside of marriage (through shame, emotional abuse, even physical abuse). But this doesn't mean believing that sex outside of marriage is wrong is the *cause* of the harm. The true cause of the harm probably lies in the manner in which people hold to their beliefs and their failure to embody other aspects of the gospel—like grace, love, and forgiveness.

All in all, the harm argument seems to describe abuses by people who hold to a traditional theology, rather than describing traditional theology itself. The traditional view doesn't tell parents to kick their gay kids out of the house, nor does it tell parents to force kids to change their orientation. There are no chapters and verses for this behavior. This is bad theology extrapolated from a warped interpretation of Scripture, nurtured by a toxic religious environment.

Third, the harm argument seems to assume that marriage and sex are essential for human flourishing—a problem we keep running into in many of these arguments. Here's what I mean. Some people who appeal to the harm argument will say something like, "If a gay person is trying to follow Jesus and is told that same-sex marriage is off the table, then this will cause massive amounts of distress, depression, anxiety, and suicide ideation."

This implies that if Jesus says we can't marry and have sex with the person we sexually desire, then following him isn't worth it. This message sounds eerily similar to so many purity messages I was raised with, where I was told that if I followed Jesus and kept myself pure, then God would bless me with an amazing spouse who would satisfy all my sexual desires. But nowhere in the Bible are marriage and sexual fulfillment built into the promises of the gospel.

The fact is, the gospel doesn't come with a promise that you will get married, fulfill your romantic desires, and live happily ever after. If this causes anyone great distress, then the root issue is not a Christian sexual ethic but the misleading assumption that God has promised us marital and sexual fulfillment. And this equally applies to marriage-crazy *straight* people just as much as to gay people considering the way of Christ. Imbibing certain cultural beliefs—*sex is a need, and I'll be miserable if I don't get married—will* make singleness or any sort of "no" to sexual desires seem impossible.

Last, I spent some time combing through several sociological studies that analyzed the experiences of gay people raised in Christian (or sometimes just religious) environments. Some of these studies are used as evidence for the harm argument. I wrote a lengthy blog post summarizing these studies, so if you want a more complete analysis, you can check it out.[7] For now, I'll just summarize some key points:

- One study looked at LGBTQ kids raised in religious (not just Christian) environments. It showed that "increased importance of religion was associated with higher odds of recent suicide

7. See Preston Sprinkle, "Is a Traditional Theology of Marriage Intrinsically Harmful toward LGBTQ People? Part 2," The Center for Faith, Sexuality & Gender, April 17, 2019, www.centerforfaith.com/blog/is-a-traditional-theology-of-marriage-intrinsically -harmful-toward-lgbtq-people-part-2.

ideation for both gay/lesbian and questioning students." It also noted that "religious-based conflict over sexual identity is often associated with conversion therapy."[8]

• Another study showed that LGBT people who identified as religious reported *higher* levels of happiness than those who didn't identify as religious. And, to the surprise of the leaders of the study, "there are no significant differences in subjective well-being between LGBT individuals who identify as evangelical Protestants ... despite that conservative denominations do not affirm same-sex relations ... compared to those who identify as mainline Protestant."[9]

• A large study was performed on gay people living in the Netherlands. It revealed that, "contrary to our expectations, younger homosexual men were at higher risk than older homosexual men comparing them to their heterosexual counterparts for suicide contemplation.... In spite of a more tolerant society in the last decades, younger homosexuals were still at high risk for suicidality." This was shocking, since the

---

8. Megan C. Lytle et al., "Association of Religiosity with Sexual Minority Suicide Ideation and Attempt," *American Journal of Preventive Medicine* 54, no. 5 (2018): 644–51.

9. M. N. Barringer and David A. Gay, "Happily Religious: The Surprising Sources of Happiness among Lesbian, Gay, Bisexual, and Transgender Adults," *Sociological Inquiry* 87, no. 1 (2016): 75–96.

Netherlands has been ranked the number one most LGBT-friendly country in the world.[10]

- Another study showed that "individuals who received religious or spiritual treatment had *higher* odds of later attempting suicide than those who did not seek treatment at all." The closest this study came to defining "religious or spiritual treatment" was its mention of "therapists who focused inappropriately on sexual orientation or who suggested that sexual minority patients should change or hide their sexual identity."[11]

- A large US study on the religious background of LGBT people showed that 83 percent were raised in the Christian church and about 50 percent left after they turned eighteen. But only 3 percent of those who left said they left primarily because of the church's theological teaching on marriage and same-sex sexual relationships.[12]

- The last study I looked at, done by the Family Acceptance Project, showed that "suicide

10. Ron de Graaf et al., "Suicidality and Sexual Orientation: Differences between Men and Women in a General Population-Based Sample from the Netherlands," *Archives of Sexual Behavior* 35, no. 3 (2006): 257–58.

11. Ilan H. Meyer, Merilee Teylan, and Sharon Schwartz, "The Role of Help-Seeking in Preventing Suicide Attempts among Lesbians, Gay Men, and Bisexuals," *Suicide and Life-Threatening Behavior* 45, no. 1 (2015): 1–12, www.ncbi.nlm.nih.gov/pmc/articles /PMC4871112/pdf/nihms785567.pdf.

12. See Andrew Marin, *Us versus Us: The Untold Story of Religion and the LGBT Community* (Colorado Springs: NavPress, 2016).

attempts nearly tripled for LGBT young people who reported both home-based efforts to change their sexual orientation by parents and intervention efforts by therapists and religious leaders (63%)." It also showed that kids who were "highly rejected" by their parents (that is, yelled at, shamed, verbally or physically abused, made fun of, etc.) are "more than 8 times as likely to have attempted suicide."[13]

These studies give us a few insights into the harm argument. First, the studies show mixed results. This should prevent anyone from making blanket statements like, "Studies show that …" followed by some ideologically driven point. The studies are mixed, sometimes contradictory. Read several studies, and then come to a more nuanced and cautious (and temporary) conclusion. Second, some of the studies are pretty broad. For instance, "going to religious or spiritual treatment" leaves so many questions unanswered: What kind of religious or spiritual treatment? I mean, both Fred Phelps of Westboro Baptist Church and my friend who's kept five hundred gay kids from suicide believe in a traditional view of marriage. But I would imagine that a gay person would have a completely different experience after hanging out with each one for about seven seconds. It's not

---

13. Caitlin Ryan et al., "Family Rejection as a Predictor of Negative Health Outcomes in White and Latino Lesbian, Gay, and Bisexual Young Adults," *Pediatrics* 123, no. 1 (2009): 346–52.

particularly helpful when studies use very broad terms like *religious environment* or *religious treatment*. Third, it seems clear that forced conversion therapy and significant family rejection lead to high rates of depression and suicidality. Fourth, one of the most careful and specific studies showed that a small percentage (3 percent) of LGBT people left their churches primarily because of its traditional theology of marriage. Many of them experienced relational, but not necessarily theological, harm. Last, the studies don't typically specify exactly what kind of posture or approach the religious environment or leader(s) embodied.

While I don't think the harm argument provides theological evidence for affirming same-sex marriage, it's absolutely true that many gay people have experienced harm in the church. Legitimate harm, not just "I heard a sermon that I disagreed with" harm. It's not enough for Christians to simply defend the traditional view of marriage and not also welcome gay people into their churches and homes and lives. Some gay people might not believe in the historically Christian view of marriage. (Many straight people don't either.) But if they don't find a warm, safe space to even consider it—one where they're listened to and loved, honored and respected, valued and delighted in—then that's the church's problem. And churches that don't create these kinds of environments will inevitably become incubators for people who end up affirming same-sex marriage.

SOME PEOPLE ARE BORN GAY, SO IT MUST BE OKAY

SUMMARY

This argument says that people don't choose to be gay; rather, they are born that way. Same-sex orientation is a fixed, innate, biologically determined part of one's humanity. It would be wrong to tell gay people that they can't be who they are or that God—who created them gay—would tell them that it's wrong to love the person they're created to love.

POINTS OF AGREEMENT

The best thing about this argument is that it affirms one of the most important truths in this whole discussion: people don't choose to be gay. Sexual attraction is not a choice. Sexual behavior is a choice. Lust is a choice. But simply being attracted to the same sex and not the opposite sex is not a choice.[1]

---

1. I'm not saying that certain social environments can't play some role in nurturing sexual attraction. I'm only saying that sexual attraction is rarely, if ever, the by-product of someone simply waking up one day and deciding that they want to be attracted to the same sex.

I can't emphasize enough how important this is. Gay people have grown so tired of hearing straight people say things like, "When did you decide to be gay?" Or, "Why don't you stop being gay?" These questions come off as both ignorant and naive. In fact, for an overwhelming number of gay people, their sexual attractions were (or sometimes still are) unwanted. According to a large study, 96 percent of gay people have prayed at least once in their life that God would make them straight.[2] Many of them spent years in agony pretending to be straight, dating people of the opposite sex, praying and praying and begging God to make them straight. The "born this way" argument resonates with the experience of so many gay people who know that they didn't simply choose to be gay.

Now, when I say "choose to *be gay*," I'm using *gay* as a synonym for being sexually attracted to the same sex. Attractions are not a choice, but sexual identities are a choice. A sexual identity (like gay or bisexual or pansexual) is a word or phrase that people use to describe themselves. Many people choose an identity that matches their actual attractions. But it's theoretically possible, for instance, for someone to label themselves as, say, bisexual since all their friends at school say they're bisexual, and not actually experience a deep, innate sexual attraction to both sexes. Or vice versa—some people are attracted to the same sex but don't choose to identify as gay. Identities are choices; sexual attraction is not. When I talk about "being gay," I'm referring to people who are

---

2. See Andrew Marin, *Us versus Us: The Untold Story of Religion and the LGBT Community* (Colorado Springs: NavPress, 2016), 116.

attracted to the same sex, regardless of whether they use the term *gay* to name those attractions.

RESPONSE

Like the previous argument, this one is so common that it's worth spending extra time wrestling with it. I'll start with an assumption that is built into the argument itself. Some say that if people were born gay, then it would be morally permissible to engage in a same-sex sexual relationship.

This logic seems solid at first, but if you think about it, it does make a bit of a leap. Inborn desires don't justify behavior. That's not really how any ethical system works. I love how gay-affirming writer Justin Lee puts it:

> Just because an attraction or drive is biological doesn't mean it's okay to act on.... We all have inborn tendencies to sin in any number of ways. If gay people's same-sex attractions were inborn, that wouldn't necessarily mean it's okay to act on them, and if we all agreed that gay sex is sinful, that wouldn't necessarily mean that same-sex attractions aren't inborn. "Is it a sin?" and "Does it have biological roots?" are two completely separate questions.[3]

---

3. Justin Lee, *Torn: Rescuing the Gospel from the Gays-vs.-Christians Debate* (New York: Jericho Books, 2012), 62.

Almost every branch of Christianity believes that people are born with desires that are in some way affected by the fall (Jer. 17:9; Eph. 2:1–3). So we can't assume that all our desires were put there by God. Even if we don't choose to experience certain desires, that doesn't necessarily mean it's okay to act on them. I mean, I don't know anyone who consistently applies the logic of "inborn desires justify behavior" to *everyone* who experiences inborn desires. Can you imagine a world where everyone is encouraged to act on their unchosen desires? We should determine what's right or wrong based on whether God determines a behavior to be right or wrong, not whether a behavior was fueled by an unchosen desire.

But what do we actually know about sexual orientation? Are some people simply born gay? This is a huge question that's received a ton of scientific attention. I'll try to be thorough without turning this into a fifty-page chapter.[4]

If by "born gay" we mean that same-sex attraction is 100 percent biological, then no, people are not simply born gay. Even though the "born this way" myth is widespread in pop culture, most scientists (secular and Christian) don't believe this. For instance, the American Psychological Association (APA) says,

---

4. I wrote a lengthy three-part blog series on this question. Part 1: Preston Sprinkle, "What Do We Actually Know about Sexual Orientation? Part 1," The Center for Faith, Sexuality & Gender, August 9, 2018, www.centerforfaith.com/blog/what-do-we -actually-know-about-sexual-orientation-part-1. Part 2: Preston Sprinkle, "What Do We Actually Know about Sexual Orientation? Part 2," The Center for Faith, Sexuality & Gender, August 16, 2018, www.centerforfaith.com/blog/what-do-we-actually-know -about-sexual-orientation-part-2. Part 3: Preston Sprinkle, "What Do We Actually Know about Sexual Orientation? Part 3," The Center for Faith, Sexuality & Gender, August 28, 2018, www.centerforfaith.com/blog/what-do-we-actually-know-about-sexual -orientation-part-3. What follows is a shorter version of those posts.

> No findings have emerged that permit scientists
> to conclude that sexual orientation is determined
> by any particular factor or factors. Many think
> that nature and nurture both play complex roles.[5]

Notice that the APA *does* say that biology (or nature) plays a role—and sometimes a very significant one—in shaping a person's sexual attractions. What the APA says is that sexual orientation can't be completely reduced to biology with no environmental influence. Both nature and nurture play complex roles, and the nature/nurture dynamic differs from person to person.

Virtually all scientists who study sexual orientation agree with the nature-and-nurture view of the APA. For instance, psychologist Lisa Diamond considers the strict "born this way" theory to be an outdated and disproven scientific theory.[6] She even called it a "myth" when I interviewed her on my podcast.[7] She finds it ethically offensive to say that same-sex unions are morally justified only if they're rooted in biology. Diamond happens to be an atheist, and she's married to a woman; she's not attacking the "born this way" myth from any kind of conservative perspective. She's just following the science.

---

5. "Sexual Orientation & Homosexuality," American Psychological Association, 2008, www.apa.org/topics/lgbtq/orientation.

6. See Lisa Diamond, *Sexual Fluidity: Understanding Women's Love and Desire* (Cambridge, MA: Harvard University Press, 2009), 19–34, 71, 74, 228–29, 231, 235–37, 239–40.

7. Lisa Diamond, "Sexual Orientation, Sexual Fluidity, and the 'Born This Way' Myth," April 19, 2021, interview by Preston Sprinkle, *Theology in the Raw*, podcast episode 859, 1:12:50, https://theologyintheraw.com/podcast/859-sexual-orientation-sexual-fluidity-and-the-born-this-way-myth-dr-lisa-diamond.

Sari van Anders, a professor of psychology, gender studies, and neuroscience at Queen's University, says, "The science of whether sexual orientation is biological is pretty sparse and full of disparate, mixed and unreplicated findings."[8] Hanne Blank, a historian of sexuality, goes even further to question the scientific credibility of the thing we call sexual orientation: "The truth is that we still don't know whether 'sexual orientation' and its subtypes can actually be said to exist from the perspective of science."[9]

Probably the largest recent study on the question of same-sex orientation was the *Science* study on genetics and same-sex behavior. It was quite a chore slugging through this one. But it too confirmed everything we've said so far:

> In the end, the scientists could not find any genetic patterns that could be used, in any way, to identify a person's sexual orientation. Instead, the predisposition to same-sex sexual behavior appeared influenced by a complex mix of genetic and environmental influences.[10]

8. Sari van Anders, quoted in Alia E. Dastagir, "'Born This Way'? It's Way More Complicated than That," *USA Today*, June 15, 2017, www.usatoday.com/story/news/2017/06/16/born-way-many-lgbt-community-its-way-more-complex/395035001.

9. Hanne Blank, *Straight: The Surprisingly Short History of Heterosexuality* (Boston: Beacon, 2012), 65.

10. Andrea Ganna et al., "Large-Scale GWAS Reveals Insights into the Genetic Architecture of Same-Sex Sexual Behavior," *Science* 365, no. 6456 (2019), https://doi.org/10.1126/science.aat7693.

Again, just because something isn't 100 percent biologically determined *doesn't* therefore mean it's a choice. I wasn't born speaking English, and yet I didn't wake up one day and choose to be an English speaker. It sure feels innate, and I can't *not* speak English. But this doesn't mean I was created by God in the womb *as* an English speaker. I wasn't "born this way."

Sexual attraction is much more complex than we often realize. In fact, we now know that sexual attraction can be quite fluid. Gay, straight, and bisexual are fine as general categories, but we shouldn't think that actual attraction is so rigidly fixed. When it comes to sexual attraction, there's more flexibility and fluidity than some people realize.

Lisa Diamond, a professor of developmental psychology at the University of Utah, performed a longitudinal study where she traced the experiences of one hundred non-straight females over a period of ten years. At the beginning of her study, 43 percent identified as lesbian, 30 percent as bisexual, and 27 percent said they didn't fit any category but were not heterosexual.

Of the 43 percent of the women identified as lesbian at the beginning of her study, 30 percent ended up pursuing full-blown romantic relationships with men (not just one-off sexual encounters),[11] and only 3 percent expressed 100 percent attractions to other women in every interview during the ten-year period.[12] In fact, Diamond found that more than two-thirds of the women she

---

11. See Diamond, *Sexual Fluidity*, 113.
12. See Diamond, *Sexual Fluidity*, 56, 146.

interviewed had changed their sexual identity at least once during those ten years. These changes went in all directions. Some women who first identified as lesbian ended up identifying as bisexual or unlabeled. Some who identified as bisexual or unlabeled later identified as heterosexual. The "unlabeled" identity became the most popular among women in Diamond's study, largely because of the unexpected fluidity in attractions they experienced over the ten years. Many women said that their ongoing experience with sexual fluidity didn't fit the rigid categories presented to them: bisexual, heterosexual, or homosexual (this was the language they used). They may have experienced seasons when their attractions felt more fixed, but then environmental changes (e.g., new relationships that stirred up unpredictable feelings) caused unexpected attractions to spring up. Some attractions were deeply emotional but not necessarily physical; others were both. Some began as emotional and led to physical intimacy, or vice versa.

To be clear, when Diamond talks about sexual fluidity, she's not talking about huge swings from being totally gay to totally straight:

> One important conclusion is that though women do, in fact, experience transformations in their sexual feelings, often brought about by specific relationships, *these changes do not appear to involve large-scale "switches" in their overall sexual orientation.* Rather, their sexual and emotional attractions typically fluctuate only within a general range.

This may mean that the overall range of a person's potential attractions is set by her orientation, but her degree of fluidity determines exactly where she will end up within that range.[13]

I repeat—*"These changes do not appear to involve large-scale 'switches' in their overall sexual orientation."* Nothing Diamond or I have said should be confused with "orientation change," even though some have taken her research in this direction. (Diamond has responded quite pointedly to this distortion of her work.)[14] Sexual fluidity typically happens within general categories of orientation.

Diamond isn't the only scholar who's shown that sexuality is often more fluid than the popular narrative would have us believe. Eric Anderson,[15] Steven Zeeland,[16] Ritch Savin-Williams,[17] Jane Ward,[18] and others have all studied female *and* male sexuality

---

13. Diamond, *Sexual Fluidity*, 160–61.

14. "Dr. Lisa Diamond: 'NARTH Distorted My Research,'" Truth Wins Out, video, 4:55, August 19, 2008, www.youtube.com/watch?v=64A2HrvYdYQ.

15. Eric Anderson, "'Being Masculine Is Not about Who You Sleep With ...': Heterosexual Athletes Contesting Masculinity and the One-Time Rule of Homosexuality," *Sex Roles: A Journal of Research* 58 (2008): 104–15.

16. Steven Zeeland, *Sailors and Sexual Identity: Crossing the Line Between "Straight" and "Gay" in the U.S. Navy* (New York: Harington Park, 1995). Zeeland himself does not identify as gay, though he says his sexual attractions "are almost exclusively" toward "active-duty or former U.S. military men," and he believes that "sexual identity is a joke" (Steven Zeeland, "A Lover of Soldiers," accessed November 29, 2022, http://stevenzeeland.com/?page_id=47).

17. Ritch Savin-Williams, *Mostly Straight: Sexual Fluidity among Men* (Cambridge, MA: Harvard University Press, 2017).

18. Jane Ward, *Not Gay: Sex Between Straight White Men* (New York: New York University Press, 2015).

and have come to similar conclusions as Diamond. The binary categories of gay and straight aren't as ironclad as many people think, as if humans can be neatly separated in terms of who they are sexually attracted to. When a straight woman makes out with another woman at a party and she enjoys it, does this mean she's bisexual? Or gay? Or just a woman who enjoyed making out with another woman? These sexual categories (gay, straight, and bisexual) might serve as helpful *thin* descriptions of typical patterns of sexual desire, but they sometimes fail as *thick* ontological descriptions of who we *are* as human beings. Sexuality is complex and, for some people, quite unpredictable.

What does all this have to do with the "born this way" argument? To put it simply: I think assumptions about sexual orientation make for weak theological arguments for affirming same-sex marriage. Ethically, it doesn't really work, since inborn desires don't justify behavior. But even the very nature of sexual attraction is complex. Some people may experience a more rigid orientation where there's little to no fluidity in their sexual attractions, while others experience unexpected and unpredictable fluidity within their general orientation. The categories of gay, straight, and bisexual might be helpful for some. But we should not think of sexual orientation as some ironed-out scientific discovery akin to Copernicus figuring out that the earth revolves around the sun.

SAME-SEX MARRIAGE IS ON THE RIGHT SIDE OF HISTORY

SUMMARY

The church has often been on the wrong side of history. From owning slaves, to mistreating women, to supporting Jim Crow laws and resisting MLK's civil rights movement—we have often failed to recognize that our views are outdated and just plain wrong. According to this argument, just as Copernicus and Galileo were persecuted by the church for coming up with a "new" view that was later found to be true, so also affirming same-sex marriage might face resistance by Christians now, but it will be taken for granted by generations to come.

Therefore, the argument proceeds, fully affirming and accepting LGBTQ people is a justice issue and part of human civil rights. To be on the right side of history and an advocate for justice is to fully support and fully affirm LGBTQ people. To believe anything different is akin to racism.

POINTS OF AGREEMENT

Several things are absolutely true about this argument. First, racism is evil and goes against the basic tenets of a Christian worldview. Second, slavery is morally reprehensible, and it's shocking that Christians in the past endorsed slavery and even owned slaves. Third, some white Christians wrongly opposed the civil rights movement and wanted Jim Crow segregation laws to remain intact. Others thought that MLK and his followers were moving too fast, which is easy to say if you're white (see MLK's "Letter from a Birmingham Jail"). Fourth, Christian history has been tainted by huge swaths of misogyny. Recent sexual abuse cover-ups by Christian leaders show that we still have a long way to go. Fifth, the church has often been on the wrong side of history when it comes to science. There are too many examples to give here. Sixth, and perhaps most relevant to our argument, the church has dehumanized, shamed, shunned, and genuinely harmed many gay people, and we should repent from any and all species of homophobia. From celebrating the AIDS epidemic as God's judgment on gay people, to forcing teens to go through conversion therapy, to encouraging parents to kick their gay kids out of the home, to preaching shame-inducing and spiritually destructive sermons that condemned gay people simply for being gay—we the church have much to repent from.

And there's more. Let me pull aside the white conservative Christians for a second. Maybe you have kids or friends using the right-side-of-history argument. You can agree with my response so far, but if we're not actually living this out, our kids won't believe us. If all our friends are white and upper middle class, if we say we oppose racism but the only time they hear us talking about race is when we denounce BLM, if we say we're not homophobic but never have any gay people into our home—our lives might testify against us. If it seems like our allegiance is to a political party more than to an upside-down kingdom, if we accuse everyone who cares about justice of being a Marxist, if we speak against critical race theory more than we do against racism, then all our talk about the traditional view of marriage will be drained of its prophetic power.

We should care just as deeply about justice, racism, and embodying the radical welcome of Christ as we do about upholding the traditional view of marriage.

RESPONSE

One of my initial concerns with the right-side-of-history argument is that it assumes history is always moving in the right direction. Not every advancement in society leads to more human flourishing. Take the sexual revolution of the 1960s, for instance. Now, I want to be clear that not everything that came out of the sixties was bad. I mean, the sixties gave us Jimi Hendrix, Led Zeppelin, and Bob Marley. Women made great strides toward equality and liberation during the sixties. And of course, the sixties ended Jim Crow segregation. There's a reason that older white men with a bad taste in music are always the ones who want to go back to the 1950s.

But the sexual revolution also separated sex from procreation, which led to much more sex outside of marriage, which led to many more kids being born without two parents. The sexual revolution encouraged people to throw off all conservative boundaries of sex, creating a much more libertine view of sexual expression. Some see this as a good thing, and there may be some good in it. But whenever the boundaries of sex are opened up, it's almost always women and children who are harmed the most. British journalist Louise Perry is one of a growing number of feminists who point out that the sexual revolution hasn't really benefited women as much as some would like to think.[1] For instance, the invention of the pill "reduced women's fear of unwanted pregnancy," which some have hailed as liberation for women. In reality, the pill enabled women "to provide the kind of sex a lot of men prefer: copious and commitment free."[2]

Evidence shows that the sexual revolution hasn't really been good for women. Rates of heterosexual anal sex have more than doubled in recent years, even though 72 percent of women experience pain during anal sex and "'large portions' do not voice this discomfort to their partners."[3] (Aside from pain, women who engage in anal sex suffer many health risks.) Rates of sexual hookups have also risen considerably, even though few women truly enjoy such commitment-free sexual relationships.[4] One of the

---

1. See Louise Perry, *The Case against the Sexual Revolution* (Cambridge, UK: Polity, 2022).

2. Kathleen Stock, foreword to Perry, *Case against Sexual Revolution*, viii.

3. Perry, *Case against Sexual Revolution*, 83.

4. See Perry, *Case against Sexual Revolution*, 82.

more common sexual practices, especially among younger people, is strangulation.[5] One study showed that more than half of eighteen- to twenty-four-year-old British women report being strangled by their male partner during sex.[6] Even though many say they consented to it, they also report being (understandably!) frightened by the act. And even though you'll hear people in the media hail strangulation as a consensual form of kinky sex, in reality it harms women while feeding some kind of power fetish of men.[7]

Once you open your eyes, it's easy to see that the sexual revolution has greatly succeeded in satisfying the sexual appetites of men while harming women and children. Such is the price to pay for progress—men will say.

Not every historical development leads to more flourishing and less harm. As the Harvey Weinstein debacle, the horrors of Jeffrey Epstein's island, and the #MeToo movement have shown, harm and abuse of women and children are just as much a problem for those who hold progressive values. Voting Democrat doesn't soften the effects of the fall on our sexual desires.

Human "progress" doesn't always lead to human flourishing.

The Industrial Revolution has brought about many amazing advancements in economics and technological development. It has also led to higher rates of isolation and overall unhappiness. Despite mind-boggling developments in technology, are humans

---

5. It's sometimes called "choking," but this is a misnomer. People can choke on food; kids can choke on Legos. Strangulation is an intentional act by another human.

6. See Perry, *Case against Sexual Revolution*, 123.

7. Perry cites a study in San Diego that reported 300 cases of strangulation, 298 of which were of men strangling women; see *Case against Sexual Revolution*, 123.

really happier today than we were in the pre-internet era? Social media has opened up all kinds of avenues to connect with people and explore a world of ideas. It's also led to skyrocketing rates of depression, isolation, anxiety, and suicidality, especially among teens. Are we on the right side of history?

History is complicated. I think it's a bit naive to think that societal progress or enlightenment always leads to more human flourishing. Renowned Harvard psychologist Steven Pinker has shown that society has improved in so many areas.[8] According to the data, there is less racism, violence, abuse, and hunger today than ever before in human history. But you have to ask yourself, Are we flourishing more today than ever before as a society?

Whether the traditional view of marriage is correct should be argued on other (theological and ethical) grounds. To my mind, it's largely irrelevant what the majority of wealthy westerners think about the issue. Simply acknowledging that most white westerners now hold to a progressive sexual ethic isn't a compelling theological argument to me.

When it comes to racism, I do get concerned with correlating the traditional view of sexual ethics with slavery or segregation laws. I mean, there's a reason that most people who do this are usually young white progressives. If you're a young white progressive, and you're quick to correlate traditional marriage with racism, I would encourage you to learn from older black people

---

8. See Steven Pinker, *Enlightenment Now: The Case for Reason, Science, Humanism, and Progress* (New York: Viking, 2018).

outside of your ideological circles to see how they feel about the analogy.

There are some similarities, of course. Black people make up a minority of people in the US, and so do gay people; both have had a minority and marginalized experience. Black people have experienced a history of oppression in America, and so have gay people (to a much lesser extent). The evangelical church has been dominated by white, male, straight voices—black and gay voices are often sidelined or never heard. One of the things I've so appreciated about my gay friends is that they have a profound sensitivity to anyone who's marginalized. Whenever I'm in a social space with a gay friend, they're almost always alert to anyone in the room who might feel out of place—people of color, neurodiverse people, or people with a physical disability.

But as I said in Foundation 2, the main focus of the historically Christian view of marriage isn't about sexual orientation. It's about sexual ethics and the meaning of marriage. This creates important points of difference between the marriage debates and racism. Sexual ethics is about moral and immoral behavior; the pigmentation of one's skin is not a moral category. Most people in the world who believe in the traditional view of marriage are people of color; most people responsible for racism and oppression in the US are white.

Some people will still say that marriage is a human right or that it's unfair for some people to be denied the chance to marry the person or persons they want. This is a provocative way of wording it, but we can't begin to wrestle with this until we first answer the question, What is marriage? We can't really talk about marriage justice until we define marriage. And personally, I'm not as interested in how any given nation might define marriage or construct laws about (the thing they call) marriage. I'm primarily concerned with how the Creator God has designed marriage and how the Christian community responds to this design. I don't see anything in Scripture that says marriage is a human right; rather, it's a theological vocation with a meaning and purpose.

To sum it up, I don't think it's helpful to consider the debates about sexual ethics and marriage through the lens of racial injustice. It's problematic on several levels, if not downright offensive to some. As the old adage goes, we should eat the meat and spit out the bones when it comes to the right-side-of-history argument. If we're going to fight against racism and injustice in the world, let's do that. And we absolutely should do that. But if we're going to consider revamping a Christian sexual ethic and the theology of marriage, then we'll need to go into another room and have a different conversation.

CHRISTIANS ARE HYPOCRITICAL

SUMMARY

Traditional Christians believe that same-sex relationships are sin, but they seem to be okay with gluttony, divorce, and heterosexual promiscuity. It's hypocritical to condemn some sins while turning a blind eye to others.

POINTS OF AGREEMENT

Christians need to own this argument, since much of it is true. We have been tolerant of some sins while condemning others. We've been lax on gluttony, divorce, and heterosexual promiscuity, and we can add to this list greed, pride, arrogance, slander, and gossip. According to some studies, about two-thirds of evangelical young people have had premarital sex,[1] about one-third have been divorced,[2]

---

1. See David J. Ayers, "Sex and the Single Evangelical," Institute for Family Studies, August 14, 2019, https://ifstudies.org/blog/sex-and-the-single-evangelical.

2. See "New Marriage and Divorce Statistics Released," Barna, March 31, 2008, www.barna.com/research/new-marriage-and-divorce-statistics-released.

and 60 percent of pastors have used porn.[3] Lesbian Christian Bridget Eileen Rivera rightly says, "Like a foul-mouthed parent who expects their child to quit cussing, the church overlooks its own promiscuity while condemning its gay members for theirs."[4]

"Yeah, but ..."

I know, I have some "Yeah, buts" too. But before we defend ourselves, we really do need to own this critique and repent from whatever it is we need to repent from. One of the unforeseen blessings of the sexuality conversation is that it has forced straight Christians to reflect on their own sins and ask the questions, "Where have we gone wrong? Where have we been lenient and hypocritical? What do we need to repent from?"

Straight Christians should be truly thankful for those who have shown us our hypocrisy. If we actually do care about holiness, then we will humbly receive this criticism.

RESPONSE

This argument isn't really an argument for same-sex marriage (at least, it shouldn't be), so there's not a whole lot we need to discuss. I mean, there's no logical, ethical, biblical reason why failing in one area (gluttony or divorce) should encourage us to

---

3. See Ron DeHaas, "What Are the Most Up-to-Date Stats on Pornography?," Covenant Eyes, updated October 25, 2021, www.covenanteyes.com/2016/01/19/what-are-the-most-up-to-date-stats-on-pornography.

4. Bridget Eileen Rivera, "A Celibate Lesbian's Cold Hard Look at Sexual Immorality in the Church," Meditations of a Traveling Nun, January 31, 2018, www.meditationsofatravelingnun.com/celibate-lesbians-look-at-sexual-immorality-in-church.

fail in another (same-sex behavior). I can't imagine Jesus looking at the church's gluttony and divorce rate and saying, "Well, since you all have really screwed up by overeating and divorcing your spouses, I think it's only fair that you reinterpret what I've said about marriage."

If someone is actually using this as an argument *for* same-sex marriage (few thoughtful people do), then it's important to truly listen to them, hear their heart, and receive the critique of hypocrisy, especially if you yourself have things you need to work on. Once you've done that, it might be helpful to ask them more about their theology of marriage: How do they define marriage? Where did they get that definition from? And how does Scripture inform that definition? That's really the heart of the theological debate.

With divorce in particular, we should acknowledge that not every divorce is against God's will. Jesus allows for divorce if there has been sexual infidelity (Matt. 5:31–32), and Paul says that if an unbelieving spouse leaves, the believing spouse is no longer bound to that marriage (1 Cor. 7:12–16). There are other complexities surrounding the divorce passages in the Bible, which we don't need to get into. While divorce isn't encouraged,[5] the Bible seems to make some allowances. But the same cannot be said of same-sex sexual behavior or sex difference in marriage. There's nothing in the Bible that views some types of same-sex behavior as permissible, while disapproving of other types.

---

5. Although, Ezra 9–10 does command divorce, but this is unique to the historical situation.

Other sins like sex outside of marriage and porn use are obviously rampant in the church. Any time we excuse or cover up such sins, that's a problem we have to own. And if churches *do* turn a blind eye to these sins, then our teaching against same-sex sexual behavior will carry little weight.

There is a difference, though, between churches that struggle with sin and churches that celebrate sin. I've never heard of a church celebrating porn or sex outside of marriage, whereas affirming churches do celebrate same-sex sexual relationships. Obviously, that's because traditional churches believe that porn and promiscuity are sins, whereas affirming churches don't believe this about same-sex marriage. It's not hypocritical if traditional churches commit sin and repent of it; it's only hypocritical if we commit sin and ... commit more sin ... and more and more, without confessing and repenting. It's one thing to struggle with sin and quite another to call sin righteousness.

All of this should bring us back to the main question at hand: whether sex difference is part of what marriage is and whether sexual relationships are designed to take place within this kind of relationship. This argument is absolutely crucial in terms of pushing the church toward repentance, humility, and holiness. But it's largely a distraction from the actual theological issues.

LOVE IS LOVE

SUMMARY

Love is one of the most basic and essential characteristics of God. "God is love," John says (1 John 4:16). And this God of love wants his image bearers to love and be loved. For centuries, this argument says, only some people were allowed to love. People of different races were barred from loving each other, as were people of the same sex. But Christianity is built on an ethic of equality and love. There is no difference between two people of the opposite sex who love each other and two people of the same sex who also love each other. Both kinds of love can be characterized by faithfulness, commitment, and sacrifice. Love is love, and elevating one kind of love above another is discriminatory and oppressive.

POINTS OF AGREEMENT

This argument can be understood and appreciated only if you climb inside someone's chest and feel their heart beat. One of our most basic desires as humans is to love and be loved, to know and be known. This argument reminds us of what it means to be human.

It also rightly highlights a central Christian virtue. The main Greek word for "love" in the Bible is *agapē*, and in its noun and verb forms, it occurs more than 250 times in the New Testament. First John 4:16 says, "God is love, and whoever abides in love abides in God" (ESV). Jesus says that loving God is the greatest command and loving your neighbor is the second (Matt. 22:37–39), and Paul says that "love is the fulfillment of the law" (Rom. 13:10).

I really want us to linger on the centrality of *agapē* love in the Christian faith. Genuine, Christlike, counterintuitive, counter-cultural, scandalous Christian love is, ironically, lacking in the Christian church. We're dividing over politics and policies, the style of music in church, or our favorite Christian authors. Issues of race, immigration, politics, and who we voted for can hardly be brought up in church without somebody chucking love right out through the stained-glass windows. "If I ... do not have love," Paul says, "I am only a resounding gong or a clanging cymbal." If I "do not have love, I gain nothing" (1 Cor. 13:1, 3). If we're not pursing the radical virtue of love, a love that includes our *enemies*, then we should probably make that a higher priority than trying to refute the "love is love" argument.

Let's make a commitment, then, to take the Bible seriously in its demands to love. Not just today or tomorrow or every other Sunday. Not just with straight people, conservative or liberal people, or your family and friends. Let's choose to love on social media, at work, and in our neighborhoods. Let's choose to love on the road when someone cuts us off. And for everything that's good and holy, let's love those across whatever side of the political aisle we're on.

RESPONSE

What does the "love is love" argument contribute to sexual ethics? The main problem is that the same Bible that talks extensively about love also talks extensively about sexual ethics. The Bible does not pit love against sexual ethics. Christians are commanded to love; they're also commanded to follow the Creator's design for sexual expression. The two are not at odds. That's because the Bible doesn't reduce love to sex.

My use of "reduce" here is important. As well intended as the "love is love" argument is, I think it cheapens both sex and love. Sex is good and holy, and God created it for a purpose. But love is so much greater than sex. To say that "love is love" to defend a particular sexual relationship is to reduce the meaning of love and limit it to a certain kind of relationship that not everyone experiences. It excludes people who aren't having sex from experiencing love. This argument rightly emphasizes love but wrongly defines it. It should go without saying that the biblical emphasis on love cannot be equated with sex. When God told us to love our neighbors, he didn't mean we should have sex with them. Love is actually, explicitly, and thankfully *not* referring only to sexual relationships. With more than 250 references to *agapē* love in the New Testament alone, no one has that kind of stamina.

I honestly don't think people who make the "love is love" argument believe they're dazzling the world with a theologically sophisticated argument for same-sex marriage. It's more of a cry from the human heart, from a person who truly does want to love and be loved, to know and be known, to spend their life with somebody they desire and not live alone. If all we do is point out that *agapē* love isn't sex, this won't satisfy the craving of the human heart. It won't help the person find true love, intimacy, and community.

If you're in a conversation with someone using this argument, it'll be much better to embody the kind of divine love they're searching for than to simply try to logically refute the "love is love" argument. Saint Augustine once said, "You have made us for yourself, O Lord, and our heart is restless until it rests in you."[1] All desires for romance, sex, and love are ultimately fueled by a quest for the Divine. So embody the love of God toward your "love is love" friend who might have just unexpectedly met God in you.

---

1. Augustine, *Confessions*, trans. Henry Chadwick (Oxford: Oxford University Press, 2008), 3.

IT'S AN AGREE-TO-DISAGREE ISSUE

SUMMARY

According to this argument, the issue of same-sex marriage is not an essential doctrine in the Christian faith but a gray area that Christians can agree to disagree on. We see similar disagreements in Scripture, even over important matters like keeping the Sabbath or observing Jewish dietary laws. Paul's pastoral advice to the "strong" and "weak" in Romans 14–15 serves as a relevant paradigm. Churches today should take a similar "third way" approach to gay marriage. Pastor Ken Wilson writes, "A third way departs from the 'open and affirming' and the 'love the sinner, hate the sin' approach by regarding the question of whether and how the biblical prohibitions apply in the case of monogamous gay relationships as a 'disputable matter' in the Romans 14–15 sense."[1] Paul prioritizes unity in the church, and so should we.

---

1. Ken Wilson, *A Letter to My Congregation: An Evangelical Pastor's Path to Embracing People Who Are Lesbian, Gay, Bisexual, and Transgender into the Company of Jesus* (Canton, MI: Read the Spirit Books, 2016), 112.

POINTS OF AGREEMENT

I used to care very little about unity in the church. I was raised in an environment where the message was, *Truth at all costs; unity if possible.* But after reading John 17, Philippians 2, and a host of other passages, I came to believe that unity *is* a significant part of orthodox Christianity.

Over the years, I've rubbed shoulders with and befriended Christians who hold many different viewpoints. Catholics and Protestants, Arminians and Calvinists, egalitarians and complementarians, Republicans, Democrats, Independents, and Christian anarchists. I have friends who affirm same-sex marriage and friends who don't. To be honest, sometimes I'm not totally sure where to draw the line. Should I hang out with Christians who deny the Trinity or believe in universal salvation? Are affirming Christians outside the bounds of orthodoxy? And if so, could we still go bowling together? (That's a joke. Affirming people don't bowl.)

I guess what I'm trying to say is, I really do enjoy hanging out with people who have diverse viewpoints. And even though I've been tested as an Enneagram One, I have a strong Nine wing, which means I just want everyone to get along.

Whenever I read writers who advocate for a third-way approach like Ken Wilson, Bridget Eileen Rivera, or Tim Otto, I really resonate with their hearts, and I think they raise some good points. In fact, I think there are several aspects of the conversation that are disputable, like identifying as gay or whether gay-affirming Christians can become members in traditional churches. While I certainly have an opinion about these questions, and I'm guessing you do too, the Bible's lack of clarity on these questions makes them disputable. There was a time in my journey when I was nearly convinced of a third-way approach to the marriage question. But after thinking it through a bit more, I've found a few problems with it.

RESPONSE

First of all, Scripture treats marriage and sexual relations as a significant part of the biblical story. We're not just dealing with a few fringe verses here and there, as some like to say. The basic essence of marriage is woven into the fabric of the creation account (Gen. 1–2), along with other primary themes like the sovereignty and intimacy of God, the goodness of creation, the full equality of men and women, and the mandate to steward God's creation with dignity and care. Intertwined with these themes is sex difference both among humans in general and in marriage in particular. This understanding of marriage becomes a way in which God reveals himself to the world, as we've seen in Foundation 2.

The third-way approach typically doesn't deal with the significance of marriage in Scripture. It usually focuses on a few prohibition passages, like Leviticus 18 or Romans 1, and points out that scholars disagree on how to interpret these.

Second, and related, some say that all of this is debated. The five prohibition passages are debated. Marriage is debated. The

Greek terms of 1 Corinthians 6:9 are very debated. Since there's so much debate over these texts, the meaning of marriage should be a secondary agree-to-disagree issue.

It's true that debate exists; lots of interpretations are debated. But guess what? The meaning of pretty much every verse in Scripture is debated. Pick up any lengthy commentary on any book of the Bible, and you'll find the author going to great pains to justify their interpretation against other scholars who disagree. I was slapped in the face with this hard reality when I entered a PhD program years ago. You know what my dissertation topic was? "The Interpretation of Leviticus 18:5b." Eighteen-Five ... B! I spent more than three years researching half a verse in Scripture. And I wasn't the only one to do so. There have actually been several studies devoted to the interpretation of this half verse. But this is more common than uncommon when it comes to biblical interpretation. Simply pointing out that debates exist over certain relevant passages about same-sex sexual relations doesn't mean there's not a clear and credible way to interpret these passages.

Now, some people just throw up their arms at all the debates and punt to the creeds, which brings us to a third thing to consider.

Early church creeds (Apostles' Creed, Nicene Creed, Chalcedonian Creed) don't contain a definition of marriage, so some people say that modern marriage debates aren't essential doctrines. This point sounds convincing at first. But if you think about it, it can cut both ways. The creeds were written in response

to various challenges to the Christian faith. There is no statement prohibiting same-sex sexual relations or the thing we now
call same-sex marriage. Why? *Because even the Christian sects
deemed heretical didn't endorse this.* No one did. Some people in
the church were engaging in same-sex sexual relations when the
creeds were written, but everyone agreed that this was sin. There
are a lot of things not mentioned in the creeds that Christians
universally would say are wrong (I'll let your mind wander).
There was simply no need to include a statement about same-
sex sexual relations in the creeds, since even the heretics weren't
advocating for this.

Speaking of creeds, fourth, the very first creed actually does
include a statement on sexuality. I'm talking about the Jerusalem
creed of Acts 15:29, which prohibits *porneia* ("sexual immorality"). As we saw in Conversation 13, *porneia* in the first century
included all the sexual sins of Leviticus 18, including same-sex
sexual relations. Acts 15 might be the most relevant passage for
this argument, since the entire chapter is all about determining
what is primary and what is secondary. The apostles clearly say
that abstaining from sexual immorality (*porneia*) is a nonnego-
tiable, a *nondisputable ethical matter.* In order for the third-way
approach to pass muster, it will need to deal with Acts 15.

Fifth, and related, the New Testament's consistent treatment
of *porneia* ("fornication, sexual immorality") makes the third-way
approach very difficult to maintain. If I can get a little personal,
it's this fifth point that first nudged me away from going full-
on third way earlier in my journey. I was exploring a third-way

approach because, to be honest, I simply wanted it to be true. A buddy of mine was catching my third-way-ish vibes, and he graciously pressed me with two questions:

"Preston, do you think that all sex outside of marriage is sexual immorality?"

"Um ... yes," I responded.

"Then do you know anywhere in the New Testament where sexual immorality is considered to be an agree-to-disagree issue?"

That drove me back to the text. I knew that *porneia* referred to all sex outside of a male/female marriage; this was well established in Judaism and early Christianity.[2] So I went home, looked up the word *porneia*, and paid close attention to how it's used. I kind of knew what I was going to see, but I wanted to be sure. I wanted to take a fresh look at the word with an eye toward the third-way approach. Here's what I found: Whenever the New Testament writers address *porneia*, they always treat it with the utmost severity. It's never considered a secondary or disputed matter. Here are a couple of statements from Paul:

> Among you there must not be even a hint of *sexual immorality* [*porneia*], or of any kind of impurity, or of greed.... For of this you can be

---

2. See Kyle Harper, "Porneia: The Making of a Christian Sexual Norm," *Journal of Biblical Literature* 131, no. 2 (2011): 363–83. Jennifer Glancy has critiqued Harper's article but not his argument that *porneia* refers to all sex outside of marriage; see her "The Sexual Use of Slaves: A Response to Kyle Harper on Jewish and Christian Porneia," *Journal of Biblical Literature* 134, no. 1 (2015): 215–29.

sure: No *immoral* [*pornos*], impure or greedy person—such a person is an idolater—has any inheritance in the kingdom of Christ and of God. (Eph. 5:3–5)

Strong words. And yes, there are other sins like greed listed too. We should absolutely avoid those as well.

Do you not know that wrongdoers will not inherit the kingdom of God? Do not be deceived: Neither the *sexually immoral* [*porneia*] nor idolaters nor adulterers *nor men who have sex with men* nor thieves nor the greedy nor drunkards nor slanderers nor swindlers will inherit the kingdom of God. (1 Cor. 6:9–10)

This one includes a general reference to *porneia* and then a specific reference to same-sex sexual relations. Again, the language could not be stronger. The next two statements are from the mouth of Jesus; a main part of his critique has to do with tolerating, teaching, or practicing *porneia*.

I have a few things against you: There are some among you who hold to the teaching of Balaam, who taught Balak to entice the Israelites to sin so that they ate food sacrificed to idols and committed *sexual immorality* [*porneia*]. (Rev. 2:14)

> I have this against you: You tolerate that woman
> Jezebel, who calls herself a prophet. By her
> teaching she misleads my servants into *sexual*
> *immorality* [*porneia*] and the eating of food sac-
> rificed to idols.... So I will cast her on a bed of
> suffering, and I will make those who commit
> adultery with her suffer intensely, unless they
> repent of her ways. I will strike her children dead.
> Then all the churches will know that I am he who
> searches hearts and minds, and I will repay each
> of you according to your deeds. (vv. 20–23)

And then, of course, we have the reference to *porneia* in Acts
15:20 and 29 mentioned above:

> You are to abstain from food sacrificed to idols,
> from blood, from the meat of strangled animals
> and from *sexual immorality*. You will do well to
> avoid these things.

As far as we can tell, every first-century Jew or Christian
would have included same-sex sexual relations under the umbrella
of *porneia*. That's why I think it's tough for Christians who believe
in traditional marriage to say this is a disputable matter. If we
believe that sex difference is part of marriage and that all sex
outside of marriage is "sexual immorality" (*porneia*), how can we
say this is a secondary issue when Scripture never does?

Some will bring up Romans 14—the famous passage about disputable matters. It's tough to sort out exactly what the believers in Rome were dividing over in this chapter. It had something to do with observing certain days as sacred, eating certain foods, and drinking wine. I've seen at least seven different scholarly attempts to determine what exactly was going on in Rome that caused Paul to pen chapter 14, and I don't claim to have all the specifics sorted out. We do know that Christian Jews and Gentiles were not getting along in the churches at Rome, so that's probably at play here as well. Most likely, the Gentiles were the "strong" believers and the Jews were considered "weak." The Gentiles probably didn't feel the need to obey all the Jewish dietary laws and observe all the special days. This doesn't mean they were going against the law of Moses but were probably going against certain Jewish traditions of the day. There were massive debates about keeping the holy days both in Judaism and in Christianity around the time Romans 14 was written.[3] Jesus himself says some pretty radical things about the Sabbath (e.g., Matt. 12:1–13), and Paul seems to say that Sabbath keeping and observing holy days isn't mandatory for Christians (Gal. 4:10; Col. 2:16).

Whatever was being disputed in Romans 14, Paul doesn't consider these to be core doctrinal issues, even though the "weaker" believers viewed them as such. Paul even considers

---

3. In Judaism, calendar debates among Jews were widespread and well documented. See, for instance, 1 Enoch, Jubilees, and the Dead Sea Scrolls (especially 4QMMT and the Temple Scroll).

these issues to be *dialogismoi,* or "opinions" (v. 1 ESV), and tells the church not to divide over them.

Ken Wilson has probably made the best case for using Romans 14 as a lens for viewing the marriage debates as disputable matters, though I ultimately don't find his argument compelling. He correlates the "strong" believer with affirming Christians who think that same-sex marriage is blessed by God, and the "weak" believer is me and those of you who think that sex difference is part of marriage. I think Wilson's framing is problematic for several reasons, but let's just go with it. Let's say that the "strong" believer parallels the affirming gay Christian and that the "weak" believer parallels the straight Christian who believes that sex difference is part of what marriage is. Paul makes it clear that the stronger believer should give up their liberty for the sake of the weaker believer (v. 21; cf. 1 Cor. 8:13). According to Wilson's logic, the gay-affirming believer should avoid a same-sex marriage relationship for the sake of not offending the weaker straight believer. The application would look something like this:

> If your brother or sister is distressed because of what you eat, you are no longer acting in love. (Rom. 14:15)

> If your brother or sister is distressed because of who you marry, you are no longer acting in love. (logical application)

Neither Wilson nor others who interpret Romans 14 this way draw this application.

Anyway, I think the parallel between what's going on in Romans 14 and the current marriage debate breaks down on several levels. First, Romans 14 is dealing with things that are nowhere affirmed as core issues in the New Testament. It has to do with matters of first-century Jewish *dialogismoi* ("opinions"), not issues related to *porneia*. Even if they *were* disputing things that were part of Old Testament law, like dietary codes, we have clear evidence from Jesus and the New Testament writers that these are no longer binding on Gentile converts. The very first Christian council in Jerusalem settled this (Acts 15).

When it comes to sex difference in marriage and same-sex sexual relationships, there was no dispute in early Judaism and Christianity. No ambiguity, no debates, no diversity—nothing. These are some of the few things that Jews from every sect— and there were several—agreed on. The Jewish-Christian New Testament writers unanimously agreed. Jews and Christians in the first century believed that certain ethical beliefs were disputable. Whether sex difference is part of marriage was not one of them.

I want to be clear that there should be no debate about whether gay/same-sex attracted people should be accepted in the church as full citizens of the kingdom. The fact that I even have to say this makes me want to throw up in my mouth, and I'm so sorry for how the church has sometimes treated these brothers and sisters in Christ. The debate is not about which temptation

people are allowed to experience. The debate is about which marriage and sexual ethic *all* followers of Jesus are called to pursue.

Second, does this mean that Christians in a same-sex sexual
relationship, which they believe is blessed by God, aren't really
Christians? Can someone be in a same-sex relationship and still
be saved? I often get asked this question, and my response always
begins with "What are their names? Where were they born? Who
are they?" My point is, I don't think it's wise to make sweeping
salvific declarations over an abstract category of people.

Now, even if I do know their names, I still don't like to speak
confidently about someone's salvific state. Only God knows, and
I'm not him. I don't know if *you* are really saved, and you don't
know if I am either. I used to run around determining everyone's
salvation, and it got so exhausting that I decided to quit. I've
known people over the years who seemed without a doubt to
be sold-out believers in Jesus but ended up leaving the faith and
becoming atheists. And in one case, an incredibly zealous mis-
sionary at a church I attended was found out to be molesting his
two daughters and went to prison for it. I've also known people
who don't look, talk, or smell very religious who, after I get to
know them, have shown me more of Jesus than any ten suit-and-
tie-wearing pastors I know. Salvation is complicated. And God
looks at the heart, not the outside. Only God truly knows.

In terms of whether someone in an immoral sexual relationship can be a Christian, here's what I would say. In light of the
passages above (and others like them), it certainly seems like the
New Testament doesn't give a lot of salvific confidence to anyone

living in ongoing, unrepentant sexual sin, gay or straight. In fact, these passages strongly condemn self-professed Christians who are living in ongoing, unrepentant sexual sin. And also, for what it's worth, some of these same passages don't give salvific confidence to people living in ongoing greed and idolatry, and the whole Bible ruthlessly condemns any confessing believer who doesn't care for the poor. Maybe you can find another way to read these passages, but to me, they just don't seem to go out of their way to make sure people living in unrepentant sin (sexual and otherwise) don't doubt their salvation. And I'll say it again: I am not talking about sexual orientation. I'm referring to anyone engaging in ongoing, unrepentant behavior that the Bible considers to be immoral.

So that's where I'm at right now. Maybe I'll refine my view after turning over new rocks that I've yet to discover; I don't know. All I know is that I'm called to love people, follow the text, speak the truth, clean out the skeletons in my own closet, and trust God to sort out the details.

THE TRADITIONAL SEXUAL ETHIC IS NOT LIVABLE FOR LGB PEOPLE

SUMMARY

The traditional sexual ethic may be biblical, but is it livable? Many gay and lesbian Christians have found it to be unlivable in the church today. This isn't because they're unwilling to pick up their cross and follow Jesus through the hard places. It's because many churches still treat gay people as second-class citizens, even if they follow a traditional sexual ethic. Or they continue to police their language ("don't call yourself gay"), exclude same-sex attracted believers from positions of leadership, or bar them from serving in kids' ministries, which whispers loud and clear—*gay people are pedophiles.*

One of the biggest things that makes the traditional ethic unlivable is the church's idolatry of marriage. The message many people hear in church is, *You're incomplete until you marry the person of your dreams*; then the church turns around and tells gay people, *You can't get married to the person of your dreams*. Both can't be true. The way the church talks about marriage and singleness makes it really hard for gay people to survive in the church, let alone flourish. The problem with the traditional sexual ethic is not that it can't be proved from Scripture. It can. The case is pretty clear. The problem is that the way the traditional church is set up makes it really hard for gay and lesbian people to live a fulfilled life.

POINTS OF AGREEMENT

This argument rings true in my own experience as I talk with gay and lesbian people in the church. The number one question I get from gay Christians exploring the traditional ethic is *not* "Is it *true?*" but "Is it *livable?*" They say, "I can live without sex, but I can't live without love and intimacy." God created us to love and be loved. Not just in the sexual sense but in the relational sense. "Many Christians *tell* LGBTQ people 'I love you,'" writes Bridget Eileen Rivera, "even as their love feels unrecognizable to anyone who has ever loved or *been* loved before."[1] Rivera goes on to tell a story of her gay friend Casey, who had a Christian friend

---

1. Bridget Eileen Rivera, *Heavy Burdens: Seven Ways LGBTQ Christians Experience Harm in the Church* (Grand Rapids, MI: Brazos, 2021), 205.

tell her she would love her "from afar." Her friend never spoke to her again.

And I can tell you hundreds of stories similar to this one.

Some straight Christians have come a long way. But so many of us are still loving gay people "from afar." We say we love, and some of us truly do. We're becoming much kinder toward gay people than we were ten years ago. But most of us are still not living out the promise of Mark 10.

In Mark 10:29–30, Jesus promises that those who have left home and family will receive the blessings of family in the church:

> "Truly I tell you," Jesus replied, "no one who has left home or brothers or sisters or mother or father or children or fields for me and the gospel will fail to receive a hundred times as much in this present age: homes, brothers, sisters, mothers, children and fields—along with persecutions—and in the age to come eternal life."

We often focus on the last part—eternal life. If we give it all up for Jesus, life may suck, but at least we get eternal life. This is a thin view of the gospel, of course, but even if it were true, it'd be worth it. To give it all up, to live a life of misery and suffering, in order to gain eternal life, would be worth it.

But Jesus doesn't say this. He says those who have "left home or brothers or sisters or mother or father or children or fields" will receive back "*in this present age*: homes, brothers, sisters, mothers, children and fields." Those who have left biological family will receive a spiritual family, the church, whose love runs thicker than blood.

I know of no other group of people today who fit this description better than gay and same-sex attracted Christians who, out of allegiance to Jesus, are committed to a life of celibacy. They've quite literally left the hope of having a biological family (and in some cases have been kicked out of their own families) in order to pursue Jesus. And Jesus promises them a reward. A reward of a spiritual family. Jesus has given them *your* home, *your* mother, *your* children and sisters and brothers and fields (economic security in the ancient world). When the church fails to embody the reward Jesus promises to celibate gay Christians, we undercut the sexual ethic we say we endorse. It's not enough to just tell gay Christians, "Don't have gay sex … Good luck with that. I'll see you on the other side." This is an incomplete sexual ethic. It's like flying an airplane with one wing. It won't work. It's not designed to work. People who leave intimate relationships are promised that they will receive even greater intimate relationships in the church.

Several years ago, I had a Zoom chat with about fifteen gay Christians pursuing celibacy. In the course of the conversation, I asked them all, "What's the most challenging thing you think about as you consider your life ahead?" Almost in unison, they all said, "Who's going to take care of me when I get old?"

Straight people with kids typically never think about this. I've got four kids, and if they don't hate me when I get old and gray (or grayer), I'm assuming that they will care for me. If my wife dies, they'll come visit me. If I can't cook my own food or care for myself, they'll take me in (or, more probably, put me in a home for seniors). I won't be totally alone, because I have a biological family.

But who's going to care for our single gay brothers and sisters when they get old? Jesus says, *I've already drawn up a blueprint for that. I've made the plans and purchased them with my own blood.* It's now up to the church to embody the promise of Jesus, to become the family, the reward, for people who have left theirs.

No celibate gay Christian should ever have to wonder, *Who's going to care for me when I get old?*

It's becoming quite common for gay Christians who once held to a traditional sexual ethic to change their view. It really does break my heart, because I don't think this change is insignificant. It's a departure from the Creator's design. But here's the thing: They rarely changed their theology simply because they suddenly found the affirming arguments intellectually compelling. They simply found the traditional church culture unlivable.

I'll never forget talking to a conservative lesbian friend of mine about this. "You know, Preston," she said, "if I ever change my view, it won't be because of the theological arguments for same-sex marriage. They're pretty unconvincing. It'll be because I just don't know how much of this oppressive conservative environment I can take." My friend was working in an evangelical context where she was constantly looked on with suspicion. Even though she was committed to a traditional ethic and a life of celibacy, people knew she was gay and they didn't know what to do with her. They kept policing her language and were lurking behind every corner, ready to pounce on some lesbian sin she had to be committing. The spotlight on her was so much brighter than on straight Christians around her. Finally it got so oppressive that she ditched it and changed her view. It really bothered me when Christians jumped on her theological change with an "Aha, I knew it!" Little did they know that their constant suspicious and judgy posture nudged her to the other side.

Some conservative straight Christians demand that gay Christians call themselves "same-sex attracted" and not "gay," even though *gay* means "same-sex attracted." Some will say, "But your gayness isn't your ultimate identity—Jesus is! He's the one who's supposed to be on the throne of your life!" To which celibate gay Christians say, "In a world that affirms my sexuality at every turn, where I can find churches that affirm same-sex marriage, where I can find many books that defend same-sex marriage by using the Bible, I'm still committing my life to celibacy because I have given my allegiance to King Jesus. You tell me where my ultimate identity lies."

Some Christians say, "I don't call myself a murderous Christian. Why should people say they're a gay Christian?" Or as one person commented on my YouTube channel, "The idea of a gay Christian makes about as much sense as a black Klansman." But being gay simply means experiencing an attraction to the same sex, and for most Christians it's an unchosen and unwanted desire. For those who commit to celibacy out of allegiance to Christ, is it really helpful or accurate to compare them to a murderer or a black member of the KKK?

My friend Greg Johnson has been a pastor for more than twenty-five years in a theologically conservative denomination. He himself is theologically conservative and passionately believes in a traditional sexual ethic. He doesn't just believe it; he lives it. He's in his early fifties, and he's never even held hands romantically with another human being. While many Christians are wondering if it's okay to go past first base with their boyfriend or girlfriend, Greg's never even fouled a ball off. All because he's given his steady allegiance to Jesus. He's literally the most sexually pure person I've ever known. And yet his denomination recently brought heresy charges against him because he experiences unwanted attraction to other guys—attraction that he's faithfully submitted to the lordship of Christ for more than thirty years of his life. "But he should *never* say he's gay! I don't call myself a murderous Christian …"

Stuff like this makes the traditional sexual ethic feel unlivable. I'm not at all saying that healthy, Christlike conversations about identity language should never be had. Some Christians raise some good points about whether it's wise to use the term *gay* as an identity label, and we should engage in such conversations with humility and genuine curiosity. But these should be actual *conversations*, not accusations.

Conversations about language (*gay* versus *same-sex attracted*) are important. And we should vigorously pursue sexual integrity according to God's design. We should take sin seriously and pursue righteousness at all costs—beginning, of course, with our own lust and greed and apathy and lack of concern for the poor. But if all straight Christians do is call gay people to say no to gay sex while failing to embody the reward Jesus promises, then we've failed. We have an incomplete ethic. Truth and love are not at odds in Scripture. If we're not loving the way Jesus did, then we're not actually being truthful. Instead of "love the sinner and hate the sin," let's love the sinner, *hate our own sin*, and invite fellow sinners to walk with us, arm in arm, toward the only one who knew no sin.

I passionately believe in the Creator's design for marriage and sexual expression, and I think the Creator has revealed this design to us clearly in Scripture. This argument doesn't actually critique a traditional theology of marriage; it critiques the manner in which the church fails to embody the holistic vision of Christ, who died to form a radical family where all kinds of people will call one another brother and sister and father and mother. When the church lives out the whole gospel of Christ, the countercultural sexual ethic of Christ actually *is* livable—and good and beautiful and compelling.

RESPONSE

(I don't want to resolve this argument for you. I want you to feel its tension—and then to live differently because of it. Be the response you long to see become true in the world: be part of God's solution to making life livable for his LGB daughters and sons.)

"This book is my fragile attempt to help us think more deeply and love more widely through a topic that sometimes lacks both."

—Preston Sprinkle

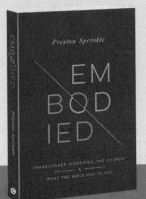

An Invitation for Christians to Join the Transgender Conversation

With careful research and an engaging style, Sprinkle explores:

- What it means to be transgender, non-binary, gender-queer, and how these identies relate to being male and female

- Why most stereotypes about what it means to be a man and woman come from culture and not the Bible

- What the Bible says about humans created in God's image as male and female and how this relates to transgender experiences

- Moral questions surrounding medical interventions such as sex reassignment surgery

- Which pronouns to use and how to navigate the bathroom debate

Preston Sprinkle (PhD) is the president of The Center for Faith, Sexuality, and Gender and a *New York Times*–bestselling author who's written a dozen books, including *People to Be Loved*, an award-winning book on faith and homosexuality. He also hosts the popular podcast *Theology in the Raw*. Preston and his wife, Chris, live in Boise, Idaho, with their four kids.

Available in print, digital, and audio
wherever books are sold